W9-AYK-213

What I Do

Jon Ronson is an award-winning writer and documentary maker. He is the author of two bestsellers: *Them: Adventures with Extremists* and *The Men Who Stare at Goats*, and a collection, *Out of the Ordinary: True Tales of Everyday Craziness*. He lives in London.

Also by Jon Ronson

THEM: ADVENTURES WITH EXTREMISTS

THE MEN WHO STARE AT GOATS

OUT OF THE ORDINARY:
True Tales of Everyday Craziness

Jon Ronson
What I Do
More True
Tales of
Everyday
Craziness

Picador

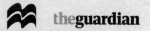

First published 2007 by Picador
an imprint of Pan Macmillan Ltd
Pan Macmillan, 20 New Wharf Road, London N1 9RR
Basingstoke and Oxford
Associated companies throughout the world
www.panmacmillan.com

ISBN 978-0-330-45373-8

Copyright © Jon Ronson 2007

The right of Jon Ronson to be identified as the
author of this work has been asserted by him in accordance
with the Copyright, Designs and Patents Act 1988.

This book is published in association with Guardian Books.
Guardian Books is an imprint of Guardian News and Media Limited.
The Guardian is a registered trademark of Guardian Media Group plc.

All rights reserved. No part of this publication may be
reproduced, stored in or introduced into a retrieval system, or
transmitted, in any form, or by any means (electronic, mechanical,
photocopying, recording or otherwise) without the prior written
permission of the publisher. Any person who does any unauthorized
act in relation to this publication may be liable to criminal
prosecution and civil claims for damages.

9 8 7 6 5 4 3 2

A CIP catalogue record for this book is available from
the British Library.

Typeset by Intype Libra Ltd
Printed and bound in Great Britain by
Mackays of Chatham plc, Chatham, Kent

This book is sold subject to the condition that it shall not,
by way of trade or otherwise, be lent, re-sold, hired out,
or otherwise circulated without the publisher's prior consent
in any form of binding or cover other than that in which
it is published and without a similar condition including this
condition being imposed on the subsequent purchaser.

Visit www.panmacmillan.com to read more about all our books
and to buy them. You will also find features, author interviews and
news of any author events, and you can sign up for e-newsletters
so that you're always first to hear about our new releases.

CONTENTS

Preface and Acknowledgements, vii

Part One: Everyday Craziness

1. Everyday Craziness, 3

2. Thinking Inside the Box, 117

3. The Chosen Ones, 140

4. Santa's Little Conspirators, 152

Part Two: How Stupid Do They Think We Are?

5. Who Killed Richard Cullen? 191

6. The Sociopath Mind Guru and the TV Hypnotist, 241

PREFACE AND ACKNOWLEDGEMENTS

Every Monday morning for the past few years I've sat in my office and pinpointed the stupidest thing I did during the previous week so I could write a *Guardian* column about it. Part One of this book collects a year's worth of these columns, from May 2006 to April 2007. (For previous years' stupidity, please see *Out of the Ordinary: True Tales of Everyday Craziness*.)

Recently, I gave a talk about my column at the Mitchell Library in Glasgow. After I'd finished someone came up to me and said, 'Would you consider yourself an unusually neurotic person?'

'Why do you ask me *that*?' I replied, narrowing my eyes and glancing suspiciously at him.

'No reason,' he said.

'No, really, why?' I said.

'Honestly, it's nothing,' he said.

'I don't believe I'm any more neurotic than you or

anyone else,' I explained. 'The thing is, we always remember the *exceptionally* stupid things we did in our lives. But the everyday craziness – the incidents I write about – are more ephemeral. Unless you take the trouble to write them down they tend to flit out of your mind as soon as they're over. Think about it: the fights you have with your spouse and children that flare up and die down in minutes, the little paranoid episodes between you and your neighbours, the crazy superstitions and petty obsessions, aren't these the ones that really count, because they mark us out as a people who spend our lives getting needlessly worked up about stupid nonsense? So we're the same, can't you see? The only difference is that I capture mine in a *Guardian* column, whereas you probably forget yours.'

'Anyway, thanks a lot, it was an interesting talk,' he said, backing away.

'Thank *you* for coming!' I called after him.

*

I also, in Part One, meet Noel Edmonds, host of the game show *Deal Or No Deal*. If anyone doubts the extent to which crazy spiritualism has permeated the hitherto secular corners of British society, they should spend a couple of days behind the scenes at *Deal Or No Deal*.

In 'The Chosen Ones' I tell the story of what happens when the children of a bunch of spiritualists are diagnosed as having attention deficit hyperactivity disorder. It is a diagnosis (or possibly a misdiagnosis) that the spiritualists do not take lying down. I suppose it is no surprise that when our leaders – in this case the medical establishment – behave irrationally, by over-diagnosing ADHD and over-prescribing Ritalin, a swathe of the public will respond irrationally by telling their children they're not hyperactive, they've instead got an overabundance of telepathy and sixth sense.

'Santa's Little Conspirators' is the story of my visit to North Pole, a Christmas theme town in Alaska. There are a lot of theme towns in the American Pacific North-West. There's a Bavarian theme town called Leavenworth, where locals dress in lederhosen and sell bratwurst. There's a Norwegian theme town called Poulsbo, where locals behave in a Norwegian way (I'm not sure how, because I haven't been there). And there's North Pole. These theme towns were established for good economic reasons. Such is the power of the out-of-town malls, downtown Leavenworth would probably be dead if it weren't for the Bavarian theme. In fact it is bustling, with tourists sitting at long tables drinking frothy beer in the afternoon sunlight while listening to oompah bands.

North Pole exists for financial reasons too. It is supposedly a place where every day is Christmas Day. It sounds in theory like a sure-fire winner. Children all over the world surely dream of visiting a town where, say, March 16th is Christmas Day, or September 29th, or even December 26th. North Pole's residents are encouraged to be Christmassy full time for the benefit of the tourists that pass through. But last year something bad happened: six of the town's thirteen-year-olds were arrested for being in the very final stages of plotting a Columbine-style school shooting.

I visited North Pole a few months later. What turned the elves bad? This is the story of what happens when a town attempts to impose a crazy dogma on its people.

In Part Two – *How Stupid Do They Think We Are?* – I meet other people who, like me, sit in offices and think a lot about the crazy ways people behave. These people, unlike me, are brilliant inventors working within the business community. They've come to realize that most of us down here are irrational and can barely cope, and they've taken it upon themselves to devise clever new ways to spot, nurture and exploit our innate stupidity on behalf of the companies that employ them.

I meet a brilliant statistician – Richard Webber –

who has invented a way for credit-card companies to precision-target with pre-approved loan offers consumers they consider to be alluringly dim-witted.

I meet a brilliant but sociopathic linguist – Richard Bandler – who has invented a way for salespeople to have the advantage over consumers by treating us as simple machines that just need a bit of reprogramming. The unnerving thing is that we *do* seem to be simple machines that will do what salespeople want us to do, if they're good at Bandler's techniques.

And I meet Wendy Cullen, whose husband, Richard Cullen, committed suicide because he was out of his depth with credit cards. Richard Cullen had been precision-targeted by the credit-card junk-mailers because they'd identified him, via a computer program, as falling within the category of 'poorly educated homeowner'.

Most of these pieces first appeared in the *Guardian*'s Weekend magazine, although I have added an epilogue here and there. Thanks to Merope Mills, Helen Oldfield, Gareth McLean, Bob Granleese and Billy Mann at Weekend, and to my last editor there, Kath Viner.

'The Chosen Ones' was commissioned by the *Guardian*'s Family supplement, so thanks to Becky Gardiner and Sally Weale.

My week in North Pole was filmed for a More4 documentary. My thanks go to Sandi Scott, Kirsty Mitchell, Peter Moore, Peter Dale, Angus McQueen, Meredith Chambers and William Grayburn, and also to Hannah Farrell and Alison Owen at Ruby films and to Katherine Butler at Film Four.

John Hodgman, Sarah Vowell, Ira Glass, Julie Snyder, Sarah Koenig and the other producers at *This American Life* have always been supportive of the thorny idea of people writing about their own domestic lives. I don't think I'd have tried it if it hadn't been for their encouragement and example. They prove it can be done well, and for good reasons.

Thanks also to Sarah Harvey, Dan Mazer, and the others at Blueprint Pictures, Laura Parfitt, Simon Jacobs, Lucy Greenwell and Caroline Raphael, who look after the *Jon Ronson On* . . . BBC Radio 4 show, Derek Johns and Christine Glover at AP Watt, Ursula Doyle, Camilla Elworthy, Richard Evans and Stephanie Sweeney at Picador, and also Amanda Posey, Nick Hornby, William Fiennes, Graham Linehan, Kate Hardie and Stevie Lee.

PART ONE

EVERYDAY CRAZINESS

1. EVERYDAY CRAZINESS

6 May 2006

My wife Elaine and I are having a weekend away. We're eating dinner in a restaurant in a country house hotel. I am, inadvertently, about to do a terrible thing.

We've been waiting for our soup for half an hour. I'm sitting there, shooting waiters paranoid, hungry glances. When it finally arrives I begin to eat it ravenously.

'Jon,' whispers Elaine. 'See that girl on the next table?'

I look up from my soup and spot a frumpy young girl, about fourteen, wearing a ball gown and sitting with her parents.

'I just saw her mimic the way you ate your soup,' whispers Elaine.

'Really?' I whisper.

'Spoiled rich cow,' whispers Elaine. 'She did this

impersonation for her parents of someone eating their soup disgustingly, and I know it was an impersonation of you because you *are* eating your soup disgustingly. It was like this . . .'

Elaine does an imitation of the girl doing an imitation of me. She twists her face, and mimes some gargoyle hunchback stuffing soup into their mouth.

'Oh, so what?' I say. 'She's only fourteen or something. How did her parents respond?'

'They *smiled*,' says Elaine.

I feel a flash of anger.

'She's hardly Gwyneth Paltrow herself,' says Elaine.

I turn back to my soup, but suddenly it doesn't taste so nice. Suddenly, my soup is a big issue.

'I'm going to the toilet,' I say.

The toilets are at the other end of a grand hallway. As I walk back to the table, I see the girl walking towards me, on her way to the toilet. It is just me and her, alone in this grand hallway.

She's *so rude*, I think. And the awful thing is, she'll never know that I know she mimicked me.

I narrow my eyes. I *have* to say something to her, I think. Maybe I should be unambiguous: 'It's not nice grotesquely to mime the way someone eats their soup.' Or maybe I should be insulting: 'I see you hunched over your food frumpily, but I don't mimic you.'

I pause. No, I think. Too much.

And then, suddenly, I know exactly what to do.

It's perfect, I think. It's simple and devastating. I'll just catch her eye and silently do an impersonation of someone eating soup disgustingly. I'll mimic her mimicking me! Not a word will pass between us. But she'll *know*. She'll know she's been caught out.

We're six feet apart now. I suddenly feel nervous about the whole thing. It is very combative, and I'm not usually a combative person.

Do it, Jon, I think. Teach her a lesson. If you don't you'll regret it.

And so I do. My heart is racing. Still, I make it look casual. I look her straight in the eye, open my mouth and rhythmically move my hand up and down, up and down towards it – clenched as if holding a soup spoon – up and down, towards my open mouth.

This is great! I think. Withering!

I shoot her a proud look as I continue my impersonation.

You'd better think twice next time you decide grotesquely to mimic the eating habits of your betters. Yes, your *betters*! I think.

The girl looks appropriately startled.

It is at this moment that the awful truth dawns on me. My impersonation of someone eating their soup disgustingly is *identical* to the way people mime blow-jobs. I am a thirty-nine-year-old man miming a blowjob to a passing fourteen-year-old girl in a hotel lobby.

Oh Jesus Christ, I think.

I stare at the ground and walk hurriedly back to our table.

'What happened?' says Elaine. 'You're shaking.'

'Shall we get the bill?' I ask.

'You're white as a sheet,' says Elaine. 'Is something wrong?'

'No,' I say.

I toy with the sugar.

If she tells her father that some middle-aged man just mimed a blowjob at her in an empty hotel hall-way, I think, I'm screwed. It's over. It's *all over*. I pause and narrow my eyes. I have to tell Elaine, I think. A normal person would chat about what had just happened in an amused, gregarious way. Only a guilty person would keep it a secret from his wife. If this ever came to court, which it won't, but if it did, the fact that I chatted about it immediately afterwards with my wife would look good in my defence.

And so I tell her.

'Oh, I'm sure she realized that your mime related to her mimicking the way you ate your soup,' she says, once I'm finished.

'Well, I'm *not* so sure,' I reply. 'She mimicked me when? An hour ago! She's fourteen. They have . . . flibbertigibbet brains. She's not going to remember what happened an hour ago. She probably thinks some man mimed a blowjob at her *apropos of nothing.*'

I glance furtively over at the next table. The girl is back, sitting with her parents. I cannot tell if they're discussing me.

I need somehow to communicate to her father the real meaning of the mime, just in case, I think. But how?

Then I have an idea.

An hour later and I'm on the terrace, drinking brandy, talking to a barrister. The girl's father is at the next table.

'And which areas of the law do you practise?' I ask the barrister.

'I don't need to practise,' he says, 'I can do it rather well by now.'

'Ha ha ha ha ha!' I say. 'So your line of work is . . .' I gregariously wave my hand as if to say, 'Do finish my sentence!' although knowing my luck with mime it probably looks like I'm offering to shove my hand up his arse.

'Crime,' he says.

'Something extraordinary happened to me tonight!' I practically yell. The barrister leans forward, clearly intrigued by the loud, exciting way I've announced the forthcoming anecdote. 'Some young girl mimicked the way I ate my soup at dinner and so when I caught her eye later I *mimed the way she mimed me eating soup*. It happened in the foyer about an hour ago! Ha!'

There's a long silence. The barrister glances quizzically at me, baffled by the weirdness of the anecdote, but I don't care. The father definitely heard.

I go to bed relieved.

It was a job well done.

16 May 2006

We're at a wedding reception in a party venue that was once a postal sorting office. They still have bits of postal equipment scattered around, but they also have a wall of discreet booths draped in velvet and linen.

'That's where the postmen used to go to have sex,' I say to my friend Alison as we pass one. Alison throws her head back and laughs. Elaine laughs, too. I am thrilled.

What a response! I think. I'll probably use that line

again when the opportunity presents itself. I pause, and inwardly decide, Yes, that small talk is simply too good to use only once.

Alison goes off to talk to someone else. I hover around the outside of the booth. 'Shall we go outside,' says Elaine, 'and get some fresh air?'

'Nah,' I say. I don't move.

Elaine looks at me. She narrows her eyes. 'Oh my God,' she says after a moment. 'You're standing here in the hope that someone will come over and talk to you so you can reuse that line of small talk about the postmen coming here to have sex.'

'I am not,' I say, adamantly.

Elaine gives me a pitying look. I take it to mean, 'Most people wouldn't dream of recycling stored-up bits of small talk at parties. Most people just come up with new funny things to say with each new encounter. But not you! What a dearth of imagination you have.'

I give her a proud, unflinching look back. It is intended to mean, 'I wasn't planning to reuse that small talk, you're wrong about that, but if I was, so what? How did society get so skewed that witty people are supposed never to say the same witty thing more than once? What kind of pressure does that put on the witty of our society?'

'Are we going outside, then?' I say casually.

'OK,' says Elaine.

We do. Outside, we chat about this and that. I bump into an old friend called Chris.

'I'm going to get a drink,' I say. 'Anyone want one?'

'I'll have wine,' says Elaine. 'No, actually, I'll have water.'

'I'll help,' says Chris.

We wander back inside. Between us and the bar lie the booths. We walk towards them. I quickly, furtively, glance behind me. There's no sign of Elaine or Alison. I can do it! The booths are upon us.

'See these booths,' I say.

'Mmm?' Chris says.

Suddenly, from the corner of my eye, I see Elaine marching towards me with alarming, almost inhuman, speed. She looks like Robocop 2. She's shouting something about wanting to have wine after all.

'Thisiswherethepostmenusedtocomeandhavesex!' I yell in a strangled voice.

There's a silence.

'What?' says Chris.

17 May 2006

An interesting-looking man has moved into our street. I invite him over for coffee.

'I'm Jon,' I say.

'I'm Sam,' he says. We look at each other.

'So what do you do?' I ask.

'I'm an actor,' he says.

'How interesting!' I say. 'What have you been in?' He tells me. 'That's great,' I say.

I pause and smile, expectantly. OK, I think. Ask me what *I* do.

'I *love* your clock!' he says. 'I'm looking for a clock exactly like that.'

I scowl to myself. Oh, I'm sure he'll ask me what I do another time, I think.

24 May 2006

I'm at the local shop with Elaine when I bump into Sam. 'Sam!' I say.

'Hi!' he says. 'Oh, I'm so sorry, I've forgotten your name.'

'Jon,' I say. 'And this is Elaine, my wife. Sam's an *actor*. Are you going to be in anything soon?'

11

'A few things,' he says.

'That's so *interesting*,' I say. There's a silence.

Ask me what I do, I think. It will open up a range of conversation possibilities. Go on. *Ask me what I do.*

'This a great local shop,' I say. 'It's especially handy when you work from home . . . like *I* do.'

I smile expectantly and cock my head. Suddenly, Sam's eyes brighten with excitement. 'They've got porcini mushrooms!' he says. He rushes to the other end of the shop to grab the mushrooms.

'He's *so* self-absorbed,' I hiss to Elaine. 'He's refusing to ask me what I do.'

'I'll tell you who's self-absorbed,' Elaine hisses back. '*You.*' Elaine mocks my voice. ' "When you work from home . . . like *I* do!" Talk about desperately trying to steer the conversation to yourself.'

'I'll tell you who's *really* self-absorbed,' I hiss. '*You!*'

'Huh?' says Elaine.

'You like the fact that my work pays for the groceries, but you don't like me *talking* about my work,' I hiss. 'You want the wheat but not the chaff. Well, I'm sorry, but sometimes you can't *have* the wheat without the chaff.'

'You're all chaff,' Elaine hisses. '*All chaff.*' She

pauses. 'Anyway,' she says. 'Perhaps he just wants to have a relationship with you that doesn't revolve around talking about work.'

Maybe she's right! I think. The first time I tried to steer the conversation to work he mentioned clocks. The second time, mushrooms. Clocks and mushrooms. Interesting. OK, I'll try talking to him about my hobbies or something. But what *are* my hobbies? I suppose I'm a keen walker, but that's just basically me moving my legs back and forward. What's there to talk about there? No. How can I get him to ask me about my work? And then I have an idea.

It is half an hour later, and I'm giving Sam a tour of my house. I show him the living room, the kitchen, the bedrooms. Finally, we come to a rest outside my office door.

Here we go, I think. I fling it open to reveal a tremendous shrine to myself: my book covers framed on the wall, photos of me with Ian Paisley and Omar Bakri Mohammed, and so on.

Sam and I stand in the midst of this. I look at him.

'Oh, you've got a Mac G5,' he says. 'How do you find it?'

1 June 2006

I'm working in Paris for the weekend and so I bring my family along. We wander through the Jardin du Luxembourg and watch people play boules. 'If we lived in Paris,' I say, 'we could play boules.'

We have lunch in a bistro.

'We should move to Paris,' I say. 'Really! Why the hell not?'

I do a carefree wave of my arm. 'We could rent our house out for a year. Enrol Joel in a bilingual school. I could write on my laptop in the Jardin du Luxembourg like I saw that man do. Just live an elegant, cerebral Parisian life for a year. Monsieur!' I call to the waiter. He ignores me.

'It's "garçon",' says Elaine.

'Are you sure?' I say. 'That doesn't seem right.'

'Really,' says Elaine. 'It's "garçon". Just shout "garçon". Shout "garçon".'

'You're *wrong*,' I hiss.

'Then we'll sit here and not get served,' hisses Elaine. There's an angry silence. 'Shout "garçon",' says Elaine.

'*Monsieur*,' I call, pointedly.

The waiter comes. 'Ah, monsieur,' I say. 'Je voudrais steak frites pour moi.' I point at my son Joel and add, 'Et un pizza pour le poisson.'

After lunch I look Elaine in the eye. 'Let's do it,' I say. There's a quiet reverence in my voice that underlines the colossal nature of what I'm about to say. 'Let's move to Paris.'

4 June 2006

I see Elaine on the computer. She's doing a Google search of bilingual schools in Paris. I stare at her. What the hell is she doing?

'You know,' she says, turning around, 'we really could move to Paris.'

'We can't move to Paris!' I say. 'I can't speak French. And we can't afford it. And we don't know anyone.'

'I've already paid the registration fee for a bilingual school,' says Elaine.

'You *know* I've always thought that if we move anywhere it should be New Zealand,' I say. 'My work is in *London*.' I pause.

'We're not moving to *Paris*,' I say.

13 June 2006

I am shopping in Marks & Spencer.

I know, I think, I'll get the ingredients to make a Caesar salad.

I buy the dressing, the Parmesan, the romaine lettuce and a sachet of croutons. Then I queue up to pay. To pass the time, I scrutinize the groceries of the woman standing in front of me, all laid out on the conveyer.

That's an awful lot of chocolates and alcohol, I think.

I stare at the back of her head.

Tonight, I think, she's probably going to binge on the chocolates and knock herself out with the booze. London really is a city of shattered dreams, I ponder. A big, relentless city full of fragile people, falling apart, alone. Or maybe she's having a children's party and the alcohol is for the grown-ups.

Then I realize that the woman behind me is doing exactly the same thing to me. She's staring at *my* groceries. I try and ignore it. But I can't. She's really staring.

I'm just going to turn around and give her a little glance, I think. A little glance to say, 'I want you to know that I am aware you're forming judgements about me based on my groceries.'

So I do. I turn and glance. And then, shockingly, she speaks.

'Ooh! Croutons!' she says.

Shocked, I grin and self-deprecatingly chuckle, 'Yes! Croutons!'

Then I turn back again to face the front. I narrow my eyes.

That was a funny remark, I think. Was she implying, 'Look at you, Mr Posh, with your sachet of prepared croutons'? What I want to know, I continue to think, angrily now, is how exactly do you expect me to make an authentic Caesar salad *without* a sachet of prepared croutons? You think I should – what? – toast bread and then chop the toast into little squares and add oil? In your inverse-snobbish mind do you somehow think that's acceptably proletarian? Or would you rather I didn't eat Caesar salad at all? Would *that* be acceptable to you? If I didn't eat Caesar salad *at all*?

But I can hardly turn back now and say all of that to her. Seconds ago I chuckled self-deprecatingly as if to say, 'Yes, the croutons *are* pretentious and I *am* pretentious by association.' If I start fighting with her now, the mood swing will make me look bizarre.

The thing that's really getting to me is that the croutons were M&S's concept, not mine. They say nothing about my character. I just picked a sachet up. The fact that she's shopping here too makes her basically the *same demographic* as me.

Yes, I think, wisely. In a way the croutons say something about her too.

I nod sagely to myself. Then I pay and go.

19 June 2006

I'm considering hiring a bookkeeper to help me manage my receipts. A bookkeeper called Eric comes over for a trial session. I leave him to it.

'Eric,' I shout after a while. 'I'm going out. Help yourself to coffee or whatever. OK, bye!'

I saunter down the stairs and practically gasp. Eric has got his coat on. He's walking towards the front door too. I realize to my horror that the two of us are equidistant to the door. And we are walking at an identical pace. If this continues unabated we'll be leaving the house at exactly the same time and will consequently be forced to walk along the road together.

Oh no! I think.

I look frantically around for something that might authentically slow me down. But there's nothing. I have my keys in my hand. My coat is zipped up. I'm clearly ready to leave. I catch Eric's eye and give him a pleading look to say, 'One of us has to stop this madness before it spirals out of control and we end up walking down the road together with nothing to say to each other.'

Think laterally, Jon, I think. I've *got* it!

'I'm just going to the toilet!' I say.

'Oh,' says Eric. 'I left something downstairs.'

I hurry up to the toilet. Eric hurries down to the kitchen.

Inside the toilet I ponder Eric's demeanour as he said he'd forgotten something. It was obviously a ruse and he felt the same way I did about us leaving together, but why? I know what Elaine would say. She'd say, 'Eric just wanted to be your friend and you made him feel small, didn't you, with your antisocial behaviour. That's why he ran back downstairs. It's just like that time we had Bill round and you sat on the Internet all night. It was the rudest thing I've ever seen anyone do.'

'I can't believe you're *still* going on about that Bill thing years after it happened,' I'd reply, before adding, with a triumphant glint in my eye, 'And the fact that you're always citing that single incident is proof that I'm only rarely antisocial.'

Anyway, Eric's demeanour throughout the incident was equally awkward. He clearly didn't want to walk with me just as vehemently as I didn't want to walk with him.

His antisocial attitude makes him interesting, I think. I can relate to that. What an interestingly antisocial self-assured person.

Now all I need to do is wait here in the toilet until I hear him scamper away.

So I do.

I'm going to hire him! I think.

1 July 2006

It's breakfast time. My eight-year-old son, Joel, comes downstairs to the kitchen.

'Can I have a Swiss Army knife?' he asks me.

'Yes, you can!' I emotionally yell.

I imagine the two of us – father and son – camping in the forest together, whittling things. Maybe one of us would get a splinter, but it wouldn't matter because Swiss Army knives have tweezers. I had a Swiss Army knife when I was a child. It was my most prized possession. I used to take it to the woods, and cut tiny things with the tiny scissors. It's a wholesome thing. It's outdoorsy.

'You're *not having a Swiss Army knife*,' yells Elaine.

She turns to me. 'You're promising a knife to an eight-year-old boy? You're going to buy him a *weapon*?'

'I . . . uh . . .' I say.

'An eight-year-old boy with a history of being fascinated by weapons?' she yells.

She's referring to the nunchucks I once rashly bought him when he was interested in Bruce Lee. The nunchucks are now out of his reach, locked away in the cupboard of presents that turned out to be not good ideas.

'I was just thinking about the two of us whittling things,' I mutter, sadly, into my cereal. Then I give Elaine a proud, defiant look, as if to say, 'You'll never understand. This is a father–son thing.'

Elaine falters a little in the wake of the look.

Ha, I think. That was a pretty unassailable look I just gave Elaine. Yes, it was a pretty powerful look. There's not much she can say in response to *that* look.

'Yes,' says Joel quickly. 'That's all I want to do. Whittle.'

At this, Elaine recovers. 'You don't even know what whittling is,' she snarls. Then she turns to me. 'When has he ever been interested in whittling? Or you, for that matter?'

'I just wanted to whittle,' says Joel, mournfully.

'See?' I say. 'He just wanted to whittle.'

But I know Elaine is right. Joel is no whittler. Still, I'm not prepared to concede defeat.

'I'm sick of you not letting me be me!' I yell. 'You know what? I'm taking Joel away for a holiday. Just the two of us. Where we can do outdoorsy things! I am!'

'Fine!' says Elaine. 'Where?'

There is a silence.

'Iceland!' I yell.

'Fine,' says Elaine. She storms out of the room. Joel and I look silently at each other.

'Actually,' Joel whispers, 'I want the knife for two things. That thing you said.'

'Whittling,' I say.

'Yes, whittling,' says Joel. 'And defending myself.'

That night, Elaine and I go to a party.

'Would you like some crisps?' the host asks me.

'No, thank you,' I reply. 'I'm going to have cereal when I get home.'

From the corner of my eye, I spot Elaine. She's

overheard this exchange of small talk and is now – for some reason – pointedly glaring at me.

'What?' I mouth at her, confused.

'Be more general,' she comes over and whispers.

'What?' I whisper back.

'Your small talk,' she whispers. 'Make it more general.'

'What?' I whisper.

'Nobody cares if you're going to have cereal when you get home,' she whispers. 'Nobody cares.'

I scowl inwardly. Personally, I don't know what was so bad about the cereal exchange. It was just basic small talk, as far as I understand the concept.

On the way home Elaine says, 'Your small talk was just inane.'

'I'm serious about taking Joel to Iceland,' I reply.

'Fine,' says Elaine.

Everything will be all right in Iceland, I think. There'll be nobody there to criticize my small talk, and Joel and I can do outdoorsy things.

I smile to myself. Yes, I think. Everything will be OK in Iceland.

1 August 2006

We are in Italy, eating in the same restaurant every night. We are now on first-name terms with the waiter, Marcello. Tonight, Marcello is being even more attentive than ever. He has, in fact, been showering me with attention from the moment we walked in. He's treating me like a man of great finesse and sophistication.

'Mr Jonathan!' he says. 'Try this bread. *Molto bene!*'

'*Grazie, grazie*, Marcello!' I reply. I nibble it. '*Bravissimo!*' I declare. Marcello looks thrilled and relieved. Elaine glares at me from across the table.

'You're embarrassing me,' she whispers after Marcello leaves. 'Just act normally.'

'I don't know what you're talking about,' I say. We fall into an angry silence.

Marcello returns. 'You *must* try the sea bass,' he says. '*Delicato!*'

'Ahhh!' I sigh, with ostentatious contentment. '*Delicato!*'

Elaine is giving me a look that says, 'Can it.'

'I'm being no more nor less enthusiastic than Marcello,' I snap in a defensive whisper after he leaves. For a moment I weigh up the possibility of accusing

Elaine of not being able to handle someone treating me as a gentleman of refinement. And that this says a lot more about her than it does about me. I narrow my eyes and wonder if I can get away with this. But I know I can't.

'*OK!*' I finally admit. 'I don't know if you've noticed, but Marcello has clearly decided to take our relationship up to the next level. And I don't know how to cope with it. I'm finding it difficult.'

'Don't fawn so much,' says Elaine. Then she mocks my voice: 'Oh, *grazie, grazie*, Marcello!'

'The thing is,' I say, despairingly, 'Marcello seems incredibly excited to see me *every time he lays eyes on me*, even if the last time was only seconds earlier on the other side of the sweet trolley.'

This seems to happen a lot to me early on in relationships. Things are trundling along fine – we've achieved a comfortable level of polite cordiality that I could quite happily live with for the rest of our lives – but then the other person decides to turn the friendliness up a gear, and I panic. Where could this end? I think. Does this person like me in an eerie, limitless way? And so I overcompensate. Now Marcello brings over the sea bass.

'*Grazie, Marcello!*' I yell.

Later, I stare at myself in the hotel-bathroom

mirror and recreate the smile I gave Marcello as the fish arrived. It is grotesque: my eyes are bulging, my grin is rictus, frozen into a fearful, pleading grimace.

Oh dear, I think.

2 August 2006

Elaine and I are eating dinner in Marcello's Italian restaurant.

'I need the toilet,' I say.

I go. Five minutes later I return and sit down in silence. Something is clearly on my mind.

'What?' says Elaine.

'OK,' I explain. 'I got as far as the outside of the toilet door, but there was no indication of whether it was locked or not. And there's no handle, just a knob.'

'So tug it,' says Elaine.

'I *did*,' I sigh, exasperated. 'But not *hard enough* to know definitively whether it was locked or just stiff.'

'Well, if someone was in there they'd have said something,' says Elaine.

'Ah! I think you're wrong,' I say. I give her a 'this is an interesting discussion' look. 'If *I'm* in a toilet and the door starts being tugged I just sit there silently until the noises stop and the person goes away. I hunker down silently until it's over.'

'Well, *you* might act that way but *normal* people don't,' mutters Elaine. '*Normal* people say, "Excuse me, but there's someone in here."'

'Yeah, right!' I snort. 'Very few people say, "There's someone in here," unless the door is practically being tugged off its hinges. People don't talk to strangers when they're in the process of defecating. It makes them feel ashamed. So the fact is, I've no idea if there's anyone in that toilet.'

We look over at the toilet door. Suddenly, something seems to snap inside Elaine.

'Why the hell didn't you *tug hard enough?*' she hisses, angrily.

'Because if someone *is* in there it would have been like a *violation*,' I hiss back. 'You don't *tug, tug, tug*. It's frightening to be on the other side of the toilet door to *all that tugging*.'

'So what *did* you do during the *many minutes* you were gone?' Elaine practically yells.

'I gave the door a tiny tug,' I say. 'Then I stood there for quite a while doing nothing. Then I put my ear to the door and I listened. I heard nothing. But it might be a thick door.'

'Go back!' hisses Elaine. 'Back. Say, "Is anybody in there?" Do it. Go.'

'*All right, I'm going*,' I practically yell. Jesus, I think.

'You'll find it's empty,' Elaine calls after me. 'A *normal* person would have said something when you tugged.'

'It *suits* you to think I'm not normal,' I hiss back. 'But in fact I AM.'

I storm to the toilet. Outside the door I clear my throat.

'Um,' I practically whisper. 'Hello?'

Silence. Then I hear a plop. An unmistakable plop. And then silence again. I nod sagely to myself and I creep away.

4 August 2006

It is our last full day on holiday in Italy. The man from Surrey on the next deckchair is reading *The Da Vinci Code*. His son is off playing with my son.

'Have you read *The Da Vinci Code*?' he asks me. 'It's wonderful. I can't put it down!'

'I didn't get past the first three words,' I reply. ' "Renowned art historian blah blah, runs down the corridor blah blah". I mean, honestly! The first rule of writing is you don't *call* someone "renowned". You portray them in such a way that leads the reader to think, Wow! He's renowned! Why that book is a success is a mystery to me. Fifty million copies! And it's crap! I wrote a conspiracy book called *Them* that's *much* better than *The Da Vinci Code* and *I* didn't sell fifty million copies.'

I shake my head sadly and gaze out to sea.

'Why *Them* didn't sell millions of copies will forever be a mystery to me,' I say. Then I turn back to him and quickly add, 'Although it *was* a success.'

5 August 2006

I'm at the Ryanair check-in queue at the airport. Elaine and Joel are in the toilet. Behind me, I hear a child's voice: 'Look! It's Joel's dad!' I recognize the voice. It is the man from Surrey's son.

'Shhh, James!' I hear the man from Surrey hiss. 'Don't disturb him!'

Oh my goodness, I think. For some reason the man from Surrey finds me difficult. Do I pretend I didn't hear them, or do I show them that I'm actually *not* difficult? The latter!

I unexpectedly spin around with a big clownish grin on my face and say, 'You can disturb me! I don't mind!'

The man from Surrey looks horrified. Just then, Elaine and Joel return from the toilet.

'Hi!' says Elaine with a relaxed smile.

The man from Surrey looks incredibly pleased and relieved to see her. But then, suddenly, he radically transforms his demeanour.

'Oh. Hi,' he says to her with chilly aloofness.

I know what he's doing, I think. He's treating Elaine with pretend indifference just to make it less obvious that he's more comfortable with her than he is with me! Oh, to know as much as I know about the fragilities of the human condition, I think, sadly, as we board the plane. Sometimes it's a burden.

The plane takes off. I drink some water. The stewardess knocks my elbow as she passes. The water spills down my chin and onto my shirt.

'Sorry,' I say.

The stewardess looks indifferently through me.

I try, and fail, to cross my legs.

'Treat people like cattle,' I mutter inwardly, 'and perhaps one day we'll start to *behave* like cattle and lash out.'

Ten minutes pass. The stewardess pushes the trolley

down the aisle towards me. She narrowly misses my arm.

That was close, I think. If she'd hit me it would have really hurt.

I've become obsessed with the stewardess. She's rude to everyone and glares at crying children. I try again to cross my legs, but it's impossible. I'm trapped.

'*Eal!*' I unexpectedly shout.

'What?' says Elaine, hurriedly pulling off her headphones.

'I let out an involuntary yelp,' I say, startled. 'It just came out.'

'Well, keep yourself under control,' mutters Elaine.

'I've never made a noise like it before!' I say.

There's a slightly awed expression on my face. I didn't know that such mysterious noises existed within me.

Finally, I manage to inch my foot out from behind the seat in front and edge it into the aisle.

That's better, I think. Now my foot can breathe.

This is the week that Ryanair has been voted 'the world's least liked airline'.

The stewardess hurtles down the aisle again, pushing the drinks trolley. She tears past me.

'Aaargh!' I yell, suddenly. 'My foot!'

'Oh no!' says the stewardess, screeching to a halt.

'You've trapped my foot between your trolley and the side of my seat,' I yell.

She jerks the trolley backwards. My foot looks disturbingly twisted.

'I'm really sorry,' she says.

'Don't worry about it,' I murmur.

'Are you OK?' Elaine asks, rubbing my arm. There's a silence.

'I feigned it!' I whisper. There's a triumphant glint in my eye.

'What?' Elaine says.

'I wasn't hurt at all!' I say. 'I faked it! I just thought, Enough is enough. I wanted to reach inside the stewardess and grab her humanity and pull it out and say, "Remember this?" So I decided to really give her a jolt and feign an injury.'

There's a silence.

'What?' Elaine says.

'OK, I realize it was a pretty extreme thing to do,' I say. 'But look at the effect it had. It was like her outer shell of meanness crumbled away in the shock of the moment to reveal her long-forgotten compassionate side.'

I need the toilet. I manage to prise myself from the seat and I head up the aisle, past rows of other squeezed and subdued holidaymakers. Even though we're all in this nightmare together, we're individually coping with it by erecting invisible force fields around ourselves, like hibernating bears.

Where did Britain's Blitz spirit go? I ruefully think. Shouldn't we be singing plucky songs to help us get through this together?

I spot the stewardess. She's in the corner at the front near the coffee machine. She's having a moment to herself and doesn't realize anybody is looking at her. She's leaning against the wall, white as a sheet, drained of energy, barely able to stand. It is 9 p.m.

She must have been flying back and forth all day. She and her fellow stewards have twenty-five minutes each end to empty the plane, clean it and fill it again. Ryanair's CEO, Michael O'Leary, has amassed a personal wealth of €466 million.

It takes a force of will for the stewardess to reach over to the tannoy, she looks so exhausted. But she does, and announces: 'We sell a range of perfumes, aftershaves, children's toys . . .'

There's someone in the toilet. I wait. Finally, a woman comes out. I extend my arm in readiness for her to hold the door open for me. But she doesn't. Even though my arm is outstretched, and I have a big, expectant 'Thanks in advance for offering me the toilet door' smile on my face, the woman resolutely closes it instead.

Strange, I think. She saw my outstretched arm. Why would she close the toilet door when she knew I'd only have to open it again?

I pause and narrow my eyes. Maybe she's *done* something in there, I think, something embarrassing that she couldn't conceal. I'm a little worried now.

I catch her eye. She looks at the floor and hurries back to her seat, her head cast downwards.

Oh dear, I think.

Anxiously, I open the toilet door, just a little at first, in case something spills or trickles or gushes out onto my shoe. But there's nothing untoward in there at all.

Funny, I think. And then, suddenly, I understand.

In closing the door, I realize, she was figuratively drawing a veil on her toilet activities. She was effectively saying, 'Whatever I did or didn't do in there is none of your business. Don't even *look* at me.' Whereas, had she held it open for me she'd essentially be saying, 'Here's the door! *I* had a poo, now *you're* going to have a poo! Our two poos have combined to form one big, shared experience. Your poo is like a *continuation* of mine!'

Yuck, I think.

Now I think about it, I bet I've never held a toilet door open for anyone. And I'm *always* holding doors open for strangers. It's in my nature. There have even been occasions when I've held doors open for people who are so far away they've had to break into a small run out of politeness to me.

Oh God, I've been *too eager*, I think, during awkward times like that. Here I am, holding the door open, and she's miles away! She's still crossing the road! Now she's broken into a jog and she's mouthing something like, 'Sorry! I'll be there in a sec! You're very kind!' And I'm standing here with a stupid gallant look on my face.

But – even so, I now realize – I've probably never in my life held a *toilet* door open for anyone. And so, here in the toilet, I have an epiphany.

If there's someone waiting outside, I think, I'm going to *hold the door open for them*!

I nod to myself and I open the door. There's a man standing there.

'Here you are!' I cheerfully say.

Together, we glance at the space I'm welcoming him into – a tiny, brown, disgusting airline cubicle. He furrows his brow, slightly taken aback, and he enters.

I cram myself back in my seat.

That was a *nice* and well-balanced thing for me to do, I think.

A few minutes pass. Then the man come back and sits on the opposite side of the aisle to me. He catches my eye and smiles at me. I smile back.

'Nice holiday?' he asks.

Oh no, I think. I've inadvertently portrayed myself as being more friendly than I actually am. And now he wants to *chat to me*.

'Yes, thanks,' I mutter.

1 September 2006

I'm in the changing room at the gym. I weigh myself.

Seventy-five kilos? I think. That's not right. Last week I was only seventy-three. Nobody puts on that much weight in a week. There must be some fault with the scales.

This is the Virgin gym, which means I have to exercise below madcap signs with exclamation marks: 'Splash!' 'Chill!' 'Mmm!' 'Pump!' and, ominously, 'Do Not Under Any Circumstances Eat The Ice In The Igloo!'

I exercise with extra vigour just in case the scales weren't malfunctioning, and then I go back to the changing room. A very fat man is walking around naked.

I don't think I've ever seen anyone that fat naked before, I think.

He glances in my direction. I hurriedly look at the floor and toy with my shoes.

Did he spot me? I think. I used to be fat myself, when I was a teenager. Had I noticed someone stare at me when I was naked, I would have been extremely upset. I pause. But I really want to look at him again, I think. Is that bad? I abhor attacks on fat people. In fact, if he were walking around in front of me clothed, I wouldn't think twice about it. But it's his *nakedness* that fascinates me.

I cautiously peer upwards. His back is turned to me.

Phew, I think. I have a good look. Incredible, I think.

I feel I've looked long enough. I wander over to the water fountain for a drink. It is situated next to the possibly malfunctioning scales. As I drink, my mind turns to other things, specifically a terrible discovery I made earlier today regarding my stash of Tamiflu. I was delighted, two years ago, when I beat the bird-flu panic and ordered a batch of Tamiflu online. While everyone else was being fobbed off with fake Tamiflu from dodgy Internet pharmacies, I had the real thing, tucked away in my medicine cabinet.

This morning it struck me that the birds will begin migrating again soon – if they aren't already – so I decided to have a quick comforting glance at the Tamiflu. It was then that I noticed the use-by date: November 2006! Unless a pandemic hits within three months, I'm in the same boat as everyone else. Great. I suppose that, like with M&S sell-by dates, I can probably safely go a few weeks into December. But what if the pandemic comes in January? What then?

Suddenly my thoughts snap away from the impending bird-flu pandemic and back to the very fat naked man. He's walking towards the scales.

It'd be great to see how much he weighs, I think. Plus, I still suspect the scales may be malfunctioning. No way did I gain two kilograms in a week! Maybe he'll say something under his breath about the scales being wrong or something. I wonder if he weighs more than twenty-five stone? That would be amazing! How can I look at him, without him noticing?

And then I realize that if I drink from the water fountain at a quite extreme angle, I should have a clear view. And so I give it a try. He climbs onto the scales. I crick my neck to a painful ninety-degree angle. The water is practically shooting up my nostrils.

And then he turns his head, and he spots me. He's caught me staring at the dial. He looks hurt.

This is terrible, I think. I should say something. I should explain that I think the scales have been malfunctioning. Yes. That's what I'll do.

'Excuse me,' I say. 'Are the scales broken?'

His eyes widen. He looks at me askance, like I've just insulted him terribly.

What? I think.

1 October 2006

An email arrives from my nice but sometimes quite frenzied friend Michael. Michael can allow his thoughts to spiral out of control. I don't mind: who *doesn't* allow their thoughts to spiral? And, anyway, he is otherwise lovely. His email is about a work colleague he hates called Graham.

'If Graham keeps treating me like a twat then I'm going to start acting like a twat and LEAVE SOME DEAD FUCKING RAT ON HIS CHAIR OR SOMETHING,' Michael writes.

'Oh, Michael,' I sigh to myself. 'You *can* be a bit mad. You really should calm down.'

I could say that to some friends but not to Michael.

If I told Michael I thought he could be a bit mad he would feel hurt and he might even respond harshly to *me*! So instead I hurriedly knock off a supportive email back: 'Michael,' I write, 'things can be fucking mad at work. He does sound like a complete idiot. I think in future just ignore him. Do you reckon?'

I press send. I'm glad I took the time to write Michael that email, I think. It was the *nice* thing to do.

An hour passes. I wonder why Michael hasn't emailed me back, I think. That's strange. And actually a little rude. I furrow my brow. Oh, I'm sure he'll email me back soon.

Another hour passes. Michael *still* hasn't emailed me back, I think. Perhaps my email didn't get sent for some reason. I suppose I should double-check my sent folder. I do. And there it is. So it *was* sent, I think. Funny. Maybe I should quickly re-read what I wrote.

I do. And that is when I see it.

Oh my God, I think. Oh, shit.

I'd written my email to Michael in a great hurry. It had taken me less than ten seconds. As a result I had, it turns out, inadvertently missed out a word – the word 'things'. My email consequently read: 'Michael can be fucking mad at work. He does sound like a complete idiot. I think in future just ignore him. Do you reckon?'

I stare at the email. And the terrible irony hits me. I'm forever insulting friends behind their backs and getting away with it. I do it all the time! And nobody gets hurt! It's fine! And here I was being *nice*. Here I was taking time out of my day to be a good and supportive friend. And it's clear what Michael's thinking: he obviously assumes that I intended to forward his email and my apparently vicious comments about him to someone else and I accidentally pressed the reply button instead.

I anxiously pace my office.

What can I do to make things better? I think. Tell him the truth – that it was probably a Freudian slip and that he really ought to calm down? Use it as an opportunity to tell Michael some difficult but important truths about himself? No, of course not. That would be ridiculous. That would inevitably result in *me* being shouted at. I furrow my brow. Then what? Do nothing? Just ignore it and never contact Michael again for the rest of my life? My eyes widen with relief. Yes! I think. That's what I'll do! I make myself a cup of tea. Never speaking to Michael again is the *perfect* solution, I think whilst sipping it.

Then I realize that, against my better judgement, I actually do need to confront this issue.

I've got it! I think. I'll pretend I'm drunk! I'll write him another email full of misspellings and left-out words! That way he'll think I was drunk last time!

That's Grahm does seem twat, I write. Seriously. Iggnore him. Had a bog lunch and am a bit drunk!!!! Ah well.

I press send.

Jon, I think. You're a genius.

9 October 2006

3 a.m. I bolt awake to hear my wife on the phone to the police. She's telling them she's just seen a hoodie dart past our window holding a computer. Then he threw it into the back of a car and screeched off, leaving the getaway vehicle's boot mat strewn across the road.

The police arrive. I didn't witness the crime so I remain in the bedroom, peering through a crack in the curtains. I see Elaine pointing sombrely at the boot mat.

In the morning, I find Elaine on the street staring at the boot mat.

'If they *really* cared about solving the crime they'd have taken this mat away for fingerprint testing,' she says.

'Boot mats don't hold fingerprints,' I patiently explain. 'You need a smooth surface.'

She knows nothing about policework, I think.

'Then what about DNA?' Elaine says.

Actually, I agree. For all we know this hoodie's boot mat could be filled with hairs and blood and semen from a thousand previous crimes. I feel a frisson of excitement as I gaze upon it, this artefact from the mysterious criminal underground. What terrible secrets has it seen? What awful things have lain upon it?

29 October 2006

A policeman telephones. They think they've caught the hoodie. I listen to Elaine's end of the conversation.

'I think he was sixteen,' she says. 'Or seventeen? . . . um . . . Eighteen?'

The expression on Elaine's face says, 'I have *no idea* what he looked like but I still have a real awe for policemen, and I realize I'm in the middle of something very important, and I'm just eager to help. So I'm saying anything. *Anything!* I'm a good person.'

I can't blame Elaine. It is an impulse I understand. Fifteen years ago I lost my mobile phone. I didn't mind. I knew I only had to invoke the promise the phone company's insurance department made to me when I took out the policy: 'Whatever happens, we'll replace it, free of charge, no questions asked,' they said. 'You can throw it in a *lake* and we'll replace it.'

A lake? I thought at the time. That doesn't seem right.

And so I called the phone company.

'What's your crime number?' the man asked me.

'There wasn't a crime,' I said. 'I lost it.'

'Without a crime number we can't replace it,' the man said.

'When I took my policy out,' I said, 'your people told me I could throw it in a *lake* and you'd replace it free of charge no questions asked. A *lake*.'

'Listen,' the man said, in a whisper. 'Call the police. Tell them it's been stolen. They'll give you a crime number. We'll give you a phone.'

'No,' I said.

'The police don't mind!' he whispered. 'It happens all the time!'

Then why are you whispering? I thought.

'The police don't mind,' he said again. 'It's standard.'

And so I did. I telephoned the police.

'Oh, no, you need to go into the station to report it in person,' they said.

And so I drove to the police station.

'I was standing on the corner of Wilmslow and Dickenson Road talking on my mobile phone,' I told the policeman behind the counter. 'Two boys appeared from nowhere . . .'

Why is he looking at me funny? I thought. Can he *see* I am lying or something? Are they trained to *see* lies?

'. . . they pulled it from my ear and ran off,' I said. 'Anyway, none of this is a problem, really. It was just kids! But I was hoping for a crime number.'

I looked hopefully at him.

'You're Jon Ronson,' the policeman said.

There was a silence. Oh fuck, I thought.

'Yes I am!' I said.

'I recognize you,' he said. 'I'll tell you what. Come back at 6 p.m. and we'll take a drive around Moss Side. See if you can spot them.'

'No, honestly,' I said. 'It really doesn't matter.'

'6 p.m.,' he said.

And so – at 6 p.m. that evening – I was driven around Moss Side in an unmarked police car.

'Is that them?' the policemen kept asking as we passed various street gangs. And, each time, I had to stop myself from yelling, 'Yes! That's them!'

My impulse was to turn every one of them in because I was, and am, on the right side of the law.

I see that same look of all-consuming keenness on Elaine's face now.

She puts the phone down.

'I wonder if they'll call me as a witness?' she says.

8 November 2006

I am at Starbucks.

'I'll have a large Americano,' I say.

Should I have a muffin too? I think. Oh, Jesus Christ I've confessed in print to committing a crime. I've confessed in print to wasting police time. Fifteen years ago. And the magazines are being printed *right now*. There's nothing I can do to stop the magazines from being distributed *all across Britain*.

I pause, and narrow my eyes. Or *is* there? I think.

No, there isn't, I think.

I glance, panicked, around me. Nice-looking people are drinking coffee and laughing together.

The police are going to arrest me, I think. And *all this will end.*

I rush home to my computer and type 'wasting police time' and 'statute of limitations' into Google. The results swirl uselessly across the screen.

I phone my mother. I tell her everything. There is a silence.

'Maybe,' she says, finally, 'you should just pop over to your local police station and tell them what's happened . . .'

'You want me to *turn myself in*?' I say.

A mental picture forms. In it, a policeman rushes into his superintendent's office clutching a copy of the *Guardian*'s Weekend magazine.

'Have you seen what Jon Ronson's written, guv?' he yells, throwing it down on the table.

'Let's get him,' the superintendent yells.

I consider my mental picture for a while.

Actually, that's unlikely, I think.

To be paranoid, I realize, means you must believe that everyone else is as interested in you as you are in yourself. Which is rarely the case.

And then, all of a sudden, I stop worrying.

Saturday comes, and I am not arrested.

12 December 2006

Sam, my neighbour, has lived here more than six months now, and he still hasn't asked me what I do. It is driving me nuts.

Ask me what I *do*, I think, whenever I see him. Ask me what I do! But he never does. He's *so* self-absorbed, I think.

Today, I spot Sam outside the window. 'Do you fancy a coffee?' I mouth.

'OK!' he mouths back.

I take him into the living room. He looks at my bookshelves. 'What a lot of Christmas cards you've got!' he says.

Yes, I think, quite proudly. I *have* had a lot of Christmas cards this year. And I haven't sent *any*! It's quite something to get so many when you don't send any. It means they *really count*. None of these people thought, Oh God, Ronson sent me a Christmas card. I'd better send him one back.

I nod to myself. Yes, I think. It's only when you don't send any Christmas cards do you learn how truly loved you are. You know what? I'm *never going to send them again*!

Actually, the truth is, I've never in my life sent any Christmas cards. And look at my shelves! They're full of Christmas cards! This is a validation of my lifelong lazy attitude regarding the sending of Christmas cards. In the end, it just didn't matter!

It's like those people who stop washing their hair and after a while their hair becomes self-cleaning, I think. There's probably *loads* of things I can stop doing.

I look at Sam. Ask me what I do, I think.

He's looking at my Christmas cards.

Maybe, I think, he'll pick one up, see that it is from a notable person, and ask me what I do. I pause. Go on, I inwardly urge. Do it! Maybe I can psychically will him to do it.

Sam's arm is hovering near the Christmas cards.

Do it! I think. He grabs one. Yes, I think.

He reads the inscription. Then he puts the card back, sits on the sofa, and drinks his coffee.

'Lovely coffee,' he says.

Who was the card from? I think. I must find out.

I try and read Sam's face, but it's inscrutable.

'Yes,' I nonchalantly say, wandering over to the bookshelves. 'The coffee *is* lovely.'

I casually pick up the card. *Happy Xmas from everyone at the Nat West Advantage Premier team*, it reads.

Damn! I think.

Then I read the card next to it.

Happy Xmas from Lloyd Piggott Chartered Accountants, it reads.

Oh my God, I think. I've been deluding myself! These cards are all from *companies I do business with*.

'I usually chuck the corporate ones away,' says Sam, from the sofa. 'They don't really count, do they?'

'I usually chuck them away too!' I say. 'I don't know what happened this year!'

'By the way,' says Sam. 'What do you do for a living?'

I pause, astonished. And then it all comes gushing out. I tell him everything. I tell him about minor awards I won years ago. I tell him that Robbie Williams admires my work. It is a torrent. I can't stop myself. I finally finish. I look exhausted.

'Anyway,' says Sam. 'I'd better go.'

'OK,' I croak.

Later, I glance at the sad, corporate Christmas cards.

It's not too late! I think. I'm going to send Christmas cards!

Until now, I have never really seen the point of sending Christmas cards. I saw how I would behave upon receiving them. I would behave uninterestedly.

Sometimes I wouldn't even bother looking at the picture at all. I really didn't care.

I'd glance inside. Oh, it's from them, I'd think.

I'd feel warmly about the sender for a couple of seconds, tops.

But, inevitably, they would annoy me. They're always falling onto the floor. We, as a society, are constantly bending over to pick them up. Why add to all that hassle by sending even more cards?

But now I don't feel like that at all!

I cycle to the *Guardian* to deliver my friend there a Christmas card. I cycle on the pavement so as not to get hit by a car. I ding my bell. Then I cycle straight into the back of an old lady.

'Sorry!' I call. Giddy as I am with self-delight, I assume she doesn't mind at all that she's just been crashed into by me, so I'm surprised to see her give me a cold-eyed scowl.

Ah well! I think. I sigh contentedly.

I reach the *Guardian*. 'I've got a Christmas card for Kate on the features desk,' I tell the security guard. 'It's Jon Ronson.'

He telephones the features desk.

'I've got a Jon Ronson?' he says.

I hate it when people say my surname as a question. What's *that* all about?

'OK,' says the security guard. 'OK. Thank you.'

He puts down the phone.

'They say she's too busy to come down,' he says. 'Just leave whatever it is here with me.'

He gives me a look that says, 'And do it without causing a fuss. OK? I'm a security guard.'

He thinks Kate was only *pretending* to be too busy to come down, I realize, startled. He thinks I'm some kind of *Guardian stalker*. Do such people exist? Well, I'm not going to add further grist to his mill by acting weirdly. I know! I'm going to show him that I'm familiar with the *Guardian* by walking around his desk to give him the card in a more informal way.

And so I do.

'JUST STEP BACK OVER THE LINE!' yells the security guard.

I almost jump out of my skin.

Sod it, I think. I'm going back to being malevolent.

15 December 2006

I'm at Chicago O'Hare airport waiting to change planes, but there's a three-hour delay. The man sitting next to me is about forty. He looks like Art Garfunkel.

'God damn these delays!' he says. 'I just want to get home to see my family.'

'So do I,' I say. 'I feel a long way away from home. Where do you live?'

'You ever hear of Park Avenue, New York City?' he says. 'I live at Number 5, Park Avenue.'

'Wow,' I say. 'That's a fancy address.' He nods. I look at his clothes. They seem expensive. We fall into a silence.

'God, I need a cigarette,' he says. 'You want to join me?'

'I've given up,' I say.

'Come along anyway!' he says. 'It'll pass the time.'

We stand up together.

He's easy company, I think. Yes, it is a little unorthodox to go off with someone you don't know and watch them smoke a cigarette, but I suppose that's the kind of thing that happens at airports.

Suddenly I feel very romantic about airports and all the mysterious people you encounter in them. We're two interesting strangers, business travellers, crossing paths, passing time together before our planes take off. We start to walk towards the kerbside smoking area.

'Let me carry your bag,' he says, suddenly.

'I'm sorry?' I say.

'C'mon!' he says, his hand outstretched. He's looking at me as if to say, 'I will take it as a personal insult if you refuse my goodwill offer.'

I am taken aback. That isn't normal. Wealthy Park Avenue businessmen don't offer to carry strangers' bags. That I know. Is this a ruse for him to grab it, yell, 'Bye!' and scarper? Surely not. There are security guards everywhere on amber alert, just dying for the opportunity to shoot someone. I'm finding this quite intimidating. I don't want to give a stranger my bag, but I feel I have no choice.

'C'mon!' he says. 'Let me carry your bag!'

Maybe it's just American hospitality, I think, with narrowed, suspicious eyes.

I hand him my bag. For the remainder of the walk I stare at it, hawklike, to ensure he doesn't slip something into it, like drugs or incriminating evidence. Finally, we reach the kerb. He says, 'Excuse me a minute, I have to phone my personal secretary to tell her about the delay. She'll have to cancel some meetings.'

He hands me back my bag, and gets out his mobile phone. I inwardly breathe a small sigh of relief that the weirdness is over. But it isn't over. It has only just begun.

An hour passes. I begin to wish he'd leave me alone.

'I've got four kids,' he's telling me, 'all in private schools. Imagine what that's costing me! But at least I earn good money. Why be shy about it? I earn *great* money. But the sacrifice is all this travelling. What's the education system like in the UK?'

Ah ha! I think. An opportunity to lighten the mood and try out my best joke.

'The man in charge of Tony Blair's education reforms is called Lord Adonis,' I say. 'Don't you think it's a bit egotistical calling yourself that?' I pause. 'It's like me calling myself King Strong!'

He looks quizzically at me. I don't get it. This is just about the funniest thing I've ever thought of, yet whenever I try it out on people, they don't laugh.

'Let me buy you coffee,' he says.

'No, honestly,' I say.

'It's on me!' he says.

He pulls out some loose change from his pocket. And before I know it, I'm drinking coffee with him.

'Let me show you a picture of my kids,' he says. He rifles through his pockets. Then his search gets more frantic. He pulls everything out of his bag.

'Oh God,' he says, a look of horror on his face. 'I can't find my wallet.' He looks me in the eye. 'You can't lend me $40?' he says. 'Actually, make it $60. Just for something to drink on the plane and a cab ride home from the airport.'

Oh, come on, I think. You went to all this trouble – three hours of grooming me – just for $60?

Suddenly, I feel very sorry for him. I thought he was a mysterious businessman but he's nothing more than a cheap con man. I give him the money.

'That's great, buddy,' he says. 'I'll get my secretary to mail it back to you as soon as I get to New York.'

'Good,' I say.

Then we catch our planes home.

(A month passes. Of course he doesn't send me the money. I'm sure he never will. I keep thinking about him. Was he a professional con man? If so, how sad to pretend to have a secretary and a Park Avenue pad. Or was he a travelling businessman who cons people for a hobby, to pass the time on his long, solitary journeys across America? He really was a mystery. I probably chew over my three hours with him more than I would usually think about $60 worth of books or movies. Just when you think life is getting same old same old, something amazing like that happens.)

28 December 2006

It is a crisp and lovely night just after Christmas. Elaine and I are on our way to a party. I have a thoughtful, faraway look on my face, as if I'm recalling a memory from long ago. I turn to Elaine as she drives. She looks back at me, and she smiles.

'Do you remember the time,' I say, 'that we were at a party in Broadstairs and you said I wasn't joining in with the conversation enough?'

Elaine narrows her eyes. 'No,' she says.

'Oh, come on,' I say. 'I was leaning up against the radiator not saying much and you hissed at me, "*Join in with the conversation more!*"'

'When was this?' Elaine asks.

'About four years ago,' I say.

Elaine thinks for a moment. Then she shakes her head.

'Oh, you *must* remember,' I say, impatiently. 'I was being quiet and you gave me a stern look and you hissed in my ear, "*You're being incredibly rude! Join in with the conversation more!*"'

Suddenly, Elaine's eyes widen. 'Oh yes!' she says. 'I remember now. What about it?'

'I had *flu*!' I snap.

'Huh?' says Elaine.

'*That's* why I wasn't talking much,' I snap. 'I had *flu*! Don't you remember? When we got home that night, I took my temperature and I had *flu*! So, you see, I wasn't being rude at all. I had flu. And nobody knew because I was *disguising it to be sociable*. I really think you should apologize to me for that.'

There's a silence.

'You always allow these things from the past to fester,' says Elaine.

'No I don't,' I say. 'But I tell you who *does* allow things from the past to fester. *You!*'

'Oh yes? Like when?' says Elaine.

'Like the time I openly licked my plate in that fancy restaurant and everyone looked shocked,' I say. 'You went on about that for *years*.'

I give her a look to say, 'Ha! See?'

'And why exactly are you bringing all this up now?' Elaine snaps.

'Because I'm not feeling very well,' I explain. 'And so when we get to the party I'm going to make it clear to everyone that if I go quiet it's not because I'm antisocial. It's because I'm ill.' I pause. 'I don't want a repeat of what happened in Broadstairs, so that's what I intend to do.'

'No you're not,' Elaine snaps. 'Someone's put a lot of effort into organizing this party, and you're going to burst in and announce that you're ill and so you won't be any fun? Yeah, right, *that's* thoughtful.'

'Well, imagine this,' I say. 'I'm chatting to someone and suddenly I become mysteriously withdrawn. What's going to go through their mind? Either, "Jon's awkward and disappointing," or, "It's my fault. I must have said something stupid to Jon." I'm sorry, Elaine, but scenario one isn't fair on me, and scenario two isn't fair on the person I'm talking to. Whereas if I just happen to mention on our arrival that I'm a bit ill, nothing bad will happen if I later become withdrawn. See?'

'Then do it!' yells Elaine. '*Do it!*'

'I'm not going to do it,' I murmur sadly to myself. 'You win.'

We reach the party. 'Hi!' says Elaine.

'How are you both?' says the hostess.

'We're fine,' says Elaine, shooting me a pointed glance.

Just bide your time, Jon, I think. Patience. Elaine is bound to leave the room at some point, and all you'll need to do is let out a small moan, just a little 'Uuuuurh', and the rest will surely follow.

'I read your column,' says a man in the corner.

'Oh, *thank you!*' I yell, suddenly feeling much better.

'Jon's been feeling a bit ill, poor thing,' says Elaine to the room.

'Oh, Elaine!' I say.

I turn to the man. 'You know what she's like from reading my columns!' I say.

2 January 2007

I am in a tense work meeting.

'The story needs to be finished by Friday,' says Adam, my boss. 'Jon. How do you intend to do that?'

Everyone looks at me. I take a breath. 'Well,' I begin. 'If I write this, this bit will work better. See?'

My colleagues smile and nod. They seem impressed by my problem-solving skills. I suddenly feel a great wave of affection for them.

Look at us! I think. Travelling through life, beginning a New Year together! My pals, Adam and Paul and Wendy. In a way I kind of love them.

I carry on talking. I'm calm and measured.

I'm good, I think.

And then, suddenly, a frighteningly powerful realization fills my head. My eyes widen as I think it.

I'm more than good, I think. I'm a genius.

I furrow my brow with the weight of my realization. But whichever way I look at it, I know it is true. I'm a genius. Just look at how well I'm doing at this meeting. Somewhere inside my brain fascinating thoughts are forming and all I need to do is open my mouth and say them. And each thought is a trouble-shooting gem.

If I wasn't a genius, I think, I wouldn't have so many important work commitments between now and Friday. I've got this, two columns for the *Guardian and* something for Channel 4. I pause. I'm going to tell my colleagues about my other commitments, I think. It'll sound impressive to them.

I take a breath. 'I just hope I have time to solve the problems before Friday!' I say. 'You wouldn't believe how many other commitments I've got! There's two *Guardian* columns. And Channel 4! Phew!'

I grin.

'Well, that's your problem, not mine,' snaps my boss, Adam. 'There's a hell of a lot of work to do for me. So my advice is you get on the phone and cancel your other commitments. If you don't, maybe you'll never have to worry about having any other commitments from me.'

'I . . . uh . . .' I stammer.

I glance, panicked, over at Paul and Wendy. For God's sake say something supportive, I think. Say something like, 'Don't worry. Jon is fully committed.' I would if either of you two were in trouble with Adam.

Actually, I wouldn't. What I'd do – and have done many times – is remain silent before rushing excitedly home to tell Elaine all about it.

'Elaine! Elaine!' I'd shout. 'You'll never guess what stupid thing Paul did!'

'What? What?' Elaine would enthusiastically reply, greeting me at the door and gazing into my eyes with love.

Recounting terrible mistakes friends make always strengthens our love, I find.

And I can see from Paul's and Wendy's silent, impassive faces that they are feeling exactly the same way about me. They're going to rush home to their spouses and fall into their arms.

'Jon would be able to postpone some of his commitments until next week,' Paul tells Adam now, 'but he can't because he's going skiing in Switzerland.'

'Oh, *is* he?' says Adam, looking at me.

I gasp. Paul! I think. What have you said?

I look at Paul. He's about sixty years old. And what am I? I'm a middle-aged man being shouted at in a meeting.

We're fighting for our lives, I think.

Adam leaves the room. I get on the phone and I cancel my other commitments.

8 January 2007

I'm in a restaurant with my friend Stephen. I take a big mouthful of food and begin to munch it meditatively. We're reading the papers in silence.

'Oh,' Stephen says, looking up. 'The playwright Patrick Marber is adapting Molière's *Don Juan* for the Donmar Warehouse. That might be interesting. I like Patrick Marber's plays. *Closer* was great. Should we go?'

There's a silence.

'*Anyone* can adapt Molière!' I snarl, unexpectedly. My eyes are aflame with hatred.

Stephen looks taken aback at my sudden ferocity.

I glance up at Stephen's quizzical face.

'It's nothing,' I say.

There is a silence.

'OK,' I sigh. 'Patrick Marber poached our nanny.'

'What?' says Stephen.

'Well, all I know,' I say, 'is that one day we were sharing her – we had her on Mondays and Tuesdays, the Marbers had her on Thursdays and Fridays – and then we went on our summer holidays, and when we came back she was working for the Marbers full time.'

'When did this happen?' Stephen asks.

'Four years ago,' I say.

Stephen bursts out laughing. I feel a flash of anger. I'm the victim, yet whenever I mention it, I'm the one who sounds like a smug fool. If Patrick Marber had stolen our TV, or kidnapped my son, it would be clear-cut. We would – as a society – know the victim from the aggressor. But not in this instance.

I know what's going through Stephen's mind: Ooh! Nanny! he's thinking. Patrick Marber! Nanny! Look at you, Mr London Media, with your *theatrical connections* and your *nanny*.

'I'm sorry if my life is a cliché to you,' I snarl, 'but the fact is, we had a nanny. We were friends with Patrick Marber. I work in the media. He poached our nanny. These things happened. OK? And just because it's a cliché doesn't mean it didn't hurt. Joel had a *bond* with Christina. A real bond.'

'And how was Joel after she left?' Stephen asks.

There's a silence.

'Fine,' I say.

Stephen is not the first person I've told. In fact I went through a stage of telling everyone – my osteopath, an American stranger I got chatting to in a bar.

I can't remember how we ended up talking about it, but I do recall her gently saying to me, 'How can you find room in your life to harbour such anger against this person?'

I looked at her, perplexed, and replied, 'I can find the time. Don't worry. I can easily set aside an hour or so here and there for feeling angry about Patrick Marber.'

'Have you ever confronted Patrick Marber about this?' Stephen asks me.

'Well,' I reply, 'shortly after it happened, I got an email from him that said, "I hear you've been spreading the fantasy that we poached your nanny. That's all it is. A fantasy. Christina left you because she didn't want to work for you anymore. Do you wonder why?"'

I pause.

'Can you *believe* that email?' I say. 'Marber's clever, see? See how *clever* he is? Because if I ever tell anyone about that email, a part of them will think, Maybe Christina didn't like Jon, and that is why she left. Well, Christina did like me! She liked me a lot! Can't you see how he's just like one of the twisted characters in his own plays? So, no, I *won't* be seeing his Molière adaptation at the Donmar. You can find someone else to go with. But I will tell you this. If his characters start playing cruel, twisted mind games with each other, as his characters often do, just remember that email he sent me.'

I pause.

'Just remember that,' I say.

There's a silence.

'You've thought a lot about this, haven't you?' says Stephen.

'No,' I say.

9 January 2007

My neighbour Sam telephones to ask if I want to go to the ballet with him.

'The *ballet*?' I say.

'Yes,' says Sam. 'I've been given two tickets. I'd love you to come.'

I hate the ballet. Plus, I'm not sure I feel ready to go to the ballet with Sam. It seems like a big step. I don't know him that well. What if we can't think of anything to talk about during the interval, and we end up in an awkward silence? *What then?*

'The ballet would be lovely,' I say.

Later, I tell my wife Elaine the whole story.

'The *ballet*?' she says. I nod, panicked.

'It'll be like that *Brokeback Mountain* incident all over again,' says Elaine.

Last year I invited a man I didn't know very well to the cinema to see *Brokeback Mountain*. Midway through the movie, I accidentally touched his leg with my hand. He recoiled and looked at me askance.

I wish I could go back to the days when Sam hadn't asked me what I did, I think. Things were better then.

On Wednesday Sam calls to check if I'm still keen to go to the ballet.

'Which ballet is it?' I ask.

'It's the English National's production of the *Nutcracker*,' he replies.

'At the Coliseum?' I ask.

'Yes,' says Sam.

'That's the one with the dancer who's in the BNP!' I say.

'I'm sorry?' says Sam.

'A journalist went undercover with the BNP,' I explain, 'and he found out that one of their members is the principal dancer in the *Nutcracker*.' I pause. 'She said she was proud to be in the BNP because they're the only party willing to stop immigration.'

'Oh, so what?' says Sam.

'If I went,' I say, 'I'd feel compelled to boo her. That's how strongly I feel. I'm sorry. I'm Jewish. I just won't have members of the far right dance for me.'

'You're kidding,' says Sam.

'No,' I say, gravely. 'I'm not prepared to allow myself to be entertained by someone from the BNP.'

'I'm not suggesting you give her a standing ovation and throw flowers at her feet,' says Sam, exasperated.

'So what should I be expected to do, as a Jewish audience member?' I ask. 'Clap?' I pause. Then I add, with solemnity, 'I'm not sure I could even *clap*.'

'How about *feel transcendent*?' says Sam, crossly. 'How about *enjoy* it?'

'And what if I did?' I say. 'Then I'd be deriving pleasure from someone who possibly hates Jews! Or at least *knows* people who do.'

'Would you feel this was if she was a Bolshevik?' snaps Sam.

'No,' I say. 'I'd be happy to have a Bolshevik dance for me.'

There's a silence.

'I'd love to do something else with you sometime, though,' I say.

'OK, bye,' mutters Sam.

He hangs up.

Phew, I think. That was a close call.

16 January 2007

It's Tuesday. I receive an ominous-sounding text from Sam.

'Can I come and see you tonight?' he texts. 'There's something we need to talk about.'

'OK!' I text back. 'Oh, I've bought a new car! It's done 16,000 miles and has had two owners in a year. Why would two people sell a car in a year? You don't think it's a jinxed car, do you?'

'7pm then?' Sam texts back.

That's a portentously terse reply, after such a chatty text from me, I think.

Relations between Sam and me have been slightly frosty since the ballet incident.

What could this be about? I think. Surely the whole ballet-invitation farrago is forgotten by now. And I haven't done anything else bad to him. Or have I? The nightmare scenario is that he's discovered that I've been writing about him in the *Guardian*, and he wants to confront me about it. I shudder. But surely not. I've covered my tracks by changing his name and a few facts about him. So what, then?

Later that evening, Sam and I sit in my living room, facing each other. And he begins.

'Jon,' he says. 'Have you been writing about me in the *Guardian*?'

'No,' I say.

There is a long silence. Sam stares at me.

'Well, I suppose a bit,' I concede. 'But always with me as the idiot. I'm the idiot! It's a weekly column about how I'm the idiot.'

'I can see that,' says Sam.

'Ha! Ha! Ha!' I say. 'Oh, it's completely harmless! It's so harmless.'

At this, Sam relaxes a little. 'By the way,' he says. 'I think it is a little strange that your new car would have two owners in a year. Why did you choose to buy that one?'

There is a silence.

'Dunno,' I murmur.

'Did you haggle them down much?' he asks.

'No,' I murmur.

'Why not?' he asks.

'Didn't think to,' I murmur.

'Ha ha ha ha ha!' Sam says. 'He saw you coming! They dream of people like you! You made his day when you walked in! Ha ha ha ha ha!'

I glance anxiously out of the window at the car.

'The airbag warning light seems to be constantly

on,' I confess. 'And whenever I turn the engine off, all the radio presets un-preset themselves.'

'Ha ha ha ha ha!' says Sam.

1 February 2007

An old lady is walking her dog down the street in front of me. The dog squats in the gutter. The woman looks down blankly at it as it relieves itself.

Go on, I think. Rifle around for a plastic bag. Clean it up.

But she doesn't. When her dog is finished, they just carry on walking.

I am shocked. My face contorts itself into a picture of shocked outrage.

This has to be the first time I've ever witnessed someone allow their dog to poo on the road and not clean it up. Well, I've witnessed hooligans do it before. When that happens I avert my eyes and hurry onwards. But this is the first time I've ever witnessed an old lady do it. And so I decide to reprimand her, to make her feel terrible about what she did.

But how? I think. I know!

I can tell I still have a look of shocked outrage. The

most withering thing to do, I think, would be to just silently hold this disgusted facial expression and walk alongside her until she notices it from the corner of her eye. That'll be devastating to her.

And so I do. My jaw hangs open. There's a complicated look of horror and sorrowful wisdom in my eyes.

Come on, notice it, I think.

We carry on walking.

This is getting ridiculous, I think. I'm craning my neck into her peripheral vision. We've been walking like this for about ten seconds. I'm in danger of losing the impact. Finally, she turns around.

'What?' she says.

'I just hope a child doesn't put its fingers in your dog's poo and then rubs it in its eyes,' I say, 'because if it does it might go blind.'

I pause for a second.

That sentence had an awful lot of 'its' in it, I think. Maybe that's why it didn't sound as withering as I'd hoped.

I'm still not sure how I'm supposed to refer to a fictional, illustrative child. All those 'its' make me sound like a man standing on a pavement saying to a stranger, 'Its its its its its.' But at the same time I can hardly say, 'I just hope a child doesn't put *his or her* fingers in your dog's poo and then *he or she* rubs it in *his or her* eyes . . .' That would just sound weird, and not at all withering.

'It's called toxoplasmosis,' I say. 'When a child goes blind by rubbing dog poo in its eyes. Toxo-plasmosis.'

'It was in the gutter,' she says.

'Even so, even so,' I say.

I walk away. I'm pleased by the rueful way I delivered that final 'even so'. That was good. I walk home happy.

2 February 2007

Yesterday I did what I always do: I woke up, pan-icked, checked my emails, worked extremely hard, played with my son Joel, watched an hour of TV, went to bed, panicked, fell asleep. Today I wake up, panic, check my emails and gasp. There's one from a man called Richard I was great friends with twenty years ago. Now he's a multimillionaire investment banker, living in a vast penthouse in Manhattan. From time to time I see him in *Vogue*, photographed at some party, a beautiful woman draped over his arm. He has a reputation for being a high-society party animal.

'Jon, mate,' he writes. 'I'm going to be forty next week! Which means you're going to be forty too soon!'

I email back: 'Richard! Wow! So great to hear from you!'

'When are you going to come and stay with me?' he emails. 'Seriously. Come to America!'

I stare at the email. What if I did? I think. What if I flew to America, arrived at his penthouse, wanted to go to bed and he wouldn't let me? What if he said, 'No, no! You can't go to bed! We're going out party-ing!' I shake my head and grimace. That would be awful, I think. I suppose I could always say to him, 'I'm really jetlagged.' He can't *make* me go partying if I'm too tired, can he?

'Elaine!' I shout downstairs. 'I've been emailed by someone I knew twenty years ago. Now he's a high-society millionaire. He's invited me to Manhattan.'

There's a silence. Oh, poor Elaine, I think. She doesn't want me to go. And who can blame her? I'll be living it up in Manhattan and she'll be stuck here doing housework. No, It's not fair on her. Well that's settled it. I'm not going.

Elaine bounds upstairs. '*Go!*' she says. There's a look of unparalleled joy on her face.

'My God,' I say. 'You really want me to go.'

There's a silence. 'No, I don't,' says Elaine.

'Well, I suppose absence does make the heart grow fonder,' I say.

'Exactly,' says Elaine. 'It does.'

'Anyway,' I say. 'I've toiled in the orchard my whole career, and now the fruit is growing, why can't I sit in the sunshine and eat an apple?'

'Eat an apple!' says Elaine. 'Let your hair down!'

For the rest of the day I keep overhearing Elaine making elaborate plans for things to do while I'm gone: parties, dinners, et cetera.

9 February 2007

I arrive at Heathrow Airport.

'Ah, Mr Ronson,' says the woman at check-in. 'I'm glad to tell you you've been upgraded.'

'No way!' I say.

This is the greatest day of my life, I think.

We land at JFK.

'Ah,' says the woman at immigration, after putting my passport through a scanner. 'You need to be processed separately.'

'How exciting!' I say.

She presses a button and a red light flashes above our heads.

Ooh, I think. Exciting.

An armed guard beckons me, and I follow her to a room full of terrified-looking Muslims and Hispanics. Immigration officers scrutinize me with mistrust.

'Sit,' says one.

This may not, after all, be exciting, I think.

Plastic chairs are nailed to the floor. Immigration officials wearing guns in holsters wander in and out, holding papers, silently peering at the thirty or so terrified-looking Muslims and Hispanics and me. There are signs everywhere saying: 'The use of cell-phones is strictly prohibited.'

I'm sure they won't mind me checking my text messages, I think. I mean, after all, I am white.

I pull my phone out of my pocket. I have six messages. I go to press 'read'.

'Hey!' yells an immigration officer from across the room. I jump in my seat. 'You aren't allowed to use your phone!' he yells.

I quickly put it back in my pocket.

A feeling of dread swells within me. I'm practically in custody, I think. They aren't even letting me *check my text messages*. Will they let me phone my *lawyer* if it turns out I'm on some kind of watch list, like Yusuf Islam?

I peer at an immigration officer. I imagine him saying to me, 'You're allowed one call. You'd better phone your lawyer.'

I don't have a lawyer, I think. Who has *lawyers*? What do people do when they're told to phone their lawyers but they don't have lawyers? Well, there's that firm of solicitors on Theberton Street who did our wills a few years ago. Are they the lawyers I'd phone if I was told I had to phone my lawyer? Who texted me? What if Joel's been hurt? That settles it. I *have* to check my messages.

And so I do. I wait until no immigration officer is looking in my direction and then, quick as a flash, like Zorro, I pull my phone out of my pocket and read the first text. And my heart sinks.

Oh my God, I think.

The text is from my friend Stephen. He writes, 'I'm sorry to tell you, but Patrick Marber has been nominated for an Oscar.'

This is terrible news. The day the column about how he poached our nanny appeared I wondered if it made him angry.

I do hope so, I thought. I allowed myself a small, excited smile at the possibility.

But I need to *know*, I thought. What's the point of making an enemy angry if you don't know for certain that they are angry? It's like that thing about the tree falling in the forest. If nobody is around to hear it crash to the ground, does it make a sound?

And so I emailed Patrick Marber. I wrote, Did my column make you annoyed?

He didn't email me back. Hmmm, I thought.

I didn't think about Marber at all for a while but then, in January, I received a few excited emails from friends who'd seen previews of his new film, *Notes On A Scandal*.

'It's TERRIBLE!' they wrote.

Yes! I thought, thrilled.

But then I saw it for myself, and was upset to discover that it was actually pretty good. My friends were just being nice. And now – I discover, as I'm stuck in a holding pen for suspicious travellers at JFK – he's been nominated for an *Oscar*.

Well, I think, nodding ruefully to myself, I suppose I can no longer hope he's unsuccessful. I just have to hope he's unhappy.

I pause. I suppose this means I have to stay up all night and watch the Oscars now, I think, to make sure that he doesn't win.

'RONSON,' yells an immigration officer.

I walk to the front. He apologizes for the delay, stamps my passport and tells me to enjoy my stay in New York.

An hour later, I arrive at Richard's Central Park penthouse. He has a chauffeur on call twenty-four hours a day. Imagine that!

'We're going clubbing!' says Richard. 'Let's go!'

'The thing is,' I say, 'I bit my tongue when I sneezed in my sleep on the plane and now it's throbbing. I'll get an early night tonight to recover and we'll go clubbing tomorrow. By the way, have you got any Bonjela?'

You're *so* handsome, Richard, I think. You are an *incredibly* handsome man.

'Jon,' tuts Richard. 'Jon! Jon! Jon! You're not Neurotic Jon here. This weekend you can be *anyone*! You can do everything you ever dreamed of! Flirt with women! Stay up all night!'

Well, I suppose I *could* flirt with women, I think. That's something I've always wanted to do.

'OK!' I say. 'We'll *hit the town*! By the way, I don't suppose you have any Bonjela?'

'That settles it!' says Richard. 'Me, you and Pete are *going clubbing*.'

'Who's Pete?' I say.

'Pete's staying in a spare room for a few weeks

while he gets himself somewhere to live,' says Richard. 'Pete!'

A good-looking young man appears from a spare room. He looks me up and down suspiciously. 'I'm Pete,' he says.

'Hi,' I murmur suspiciously back. 'I'm Jon.'

I'm not sure I like the look of Pete, I think. I preferred it when it was just me and Richard.

An hour later, Richard, Pete and I are in an upmarket nightclub. The music is pumping, the lights flashing. Beautiful women, attracted by the fabulous Richard, surround us. I'm feeling heady with adrenalin and jetlag. I'm also drunk.

I'm thirty-nine and I *never* do this! I think. This is great! Neurotic Jon can stay at home and worry his life away about stupid shit. *Clubby* Jon is in town now! And he's here to *stay*! I just wish my tongue wasn't throbbing. Why didn't Richard respond to my repeated requests for Bonjela? Maybe, in his world, things like throbbing tongues just don't matter! It's like a higher plane of hedonism. They just *enjoy life*!

I shoot everyone around me an excited grin. Then I dance. I dance like a brilliant, crazy shaman. I'm lost in the music, and I love it. Yeah! I think. Yeaaaaah!

Then a young girl, about twenty, asks me for my telephone number.

'Sure!' I say.

I hear a peal of laughter coming from Pete. 'What a night!' he's loudly saying to Richard. 'Women are even asking *Jon* for his phone number! Ha ha ha!'

I peer at Pete. What's *that* supposed to mean? I think. I'll get you back for that, Pete. At some point during this weekend, I'll get you back. And my revenge, whatever it'll be, will be brilliant. Don't underestimate my power when it comes to getting back at people about things. I look at Richard. In a way I kind of love you, I think.

We arrive back at Richard's penthouse at 5 a.m.

'I had a great night,' I say. I look Richard in the eyes. 'Thank you,' I say.

Richard goes to bed. Pete and I sit alone, sipping coffee.

'Richard's great, isn't he?' I say.

'Yeah,' says Pete. 'The only thing that annoys me about him is he's got this habit of surrounding himself with people who aren't threatening to him.'

'What do you mean?' I ask.

'Oh, you know,' says Pete. 'Richard likes to be with people who don't match up to him.'

I'm going to get you back for that, I think. And when I do, you'll know it.

12 February 2007

In the end I decided not to take revenge on Pete.

Oh, live and let live, I thought. It was a lovely weekend. Now I'm on the plane home.

I suddenly feel extremely remorseful about revealing how badly I took the news that my enemy, the screenwriter Patrick Marber, had been nominated for an Oscar.

How could I write that terrible thing about hoping he's unhappy? I think now, mid-Atlantic, the blood rushing to my cheeks. I don't mind so much that I *thought* it – bad thoughts sometimes pop into the heads of good people, that's one of life's incredible truths – but it was cruel to write it. I don't wish him unhappiness. Well, I suppose if he actually wins the Oscar I'll want him to be unhappy – nobody can blame me for *that* – but otherwise I sincerely wish him well.

As soon as this plane lands, I'll text him an apology.

I nod to myself. Thank goodness I'm flying American, I think, an airline that lets you use your phone whilst taxiing on the runway. I need to apologize to him *as soon as I can*. Isn't it strange that AA lets you use your phone during taxiing but BA doesn't? What's *that* all about?

What *is* that all about? A month ago I flew BA and as we landed I thought, Yes, the stewardess has just announced that we're not allowed to use our phones until after we've cleared immigration, but AA allows it whilst taxiing, so why should BA object? No, I concluded, it is clearly perfectly fine for me to use my phone whilst taxiing in this BA plane.

And so, the moment we landed, I turned on my phone.

Even though I'm doing nothing wrong, I thought, I'd better hide it under my jacket. I did. I just need to press the 'read messages' button in the split-second between the 'you have unread messages' sign coming onto the screen and the phone making that ping-ing noise, I thought. That way I'll silence the pinging before it occurs. Even though I'm doing nothing wrong, I don't want anyone hearing that pinging noise.

And so I poised my finger in concentrated readi-ness. I was like a martial-arts sensei, my poised finger ready to hurtle downwards during that crucial fraction of a second.

Focus, Jon, I thought. Any second . . .

Then my phone made a loud pinging noise.

'Turn your phone off!' yelled the nearby steward-ess. 'We're crossing a *live runway*!'

It is a month later and I still feel embarrassed about being shouted at by that BA stewardess.

Is it too much to ask, I think, miserably, for some kind of cross-corporate continuity on this issue? Why should perfectly acceptable behaviour on one airline be a terrible crime on another? It's like being allowed to – I don't know – spit on the floor at Costa coffee but not at Starbucks. What? Has AA fitted some special phone-ray-tampering-with-the-navigational-equipment shield in the cockpit that other airlines don't have? I snort to myself. I think not! They haven't even got decent movies! Anyway, at least I know I'll be able to text Marber an apology as soon as we land.

The plane descends into Heathrow.

At what moment during the landing does it become safe to turn on my phone? I wonder. We really ought to be given some kind of directive about this. Is it the instant the wheels hit the ground? Surely not. So is it during or after that weird bit when your book flies off the armrest and goes under the seat in front? I frown. In the absence of an official directive, I have to assume it's just after that bit.

And so that's when I turn on my phone. I text Patrick Marber to say I'm sorry I wished unhappiness on him in print and congrats on the Oscar nomination. He doesn't respond.

15 February 2007

I've been invited to chair an important debate on racism to mark the anniversary of the founding of the Commission for Racial Equality.

'You're not going to do it, are you?' says Elaine. 'It doesn't sound like your sort of thing.'

'It *is* my sort of thing,' I reply.

What does she mean by that? I think.

'Anyway,' I say, 'I've got a brilliant opening line: "I feel funny chairing a debate on racism. On the one hand I'm Jewish, which makes me a minority. But, then again, we *control* the media!"' Elaine laughs.

'It just popped into my head!' I say.

I walk to the debate, inwardly practising my opening joke over and over.

What if I'm *over*-rehearsing it? I think. Knowing my luck, now I've over-rehearsed it, I'll stumble over the words. I furrow my brow.

An hour later: the room is full of campaigners

against racism, school parties of teenagers for whom racism is a very real daily issue, MPs and media people. I'm on stage with the panellists. I clear my throat.

'I feel funny chairing a debate on racism,' I begin. 'On the one hand I'm Jewish . . .'

Nearly there, I think. Keep level-headed and you won't blow it.

'. . . which makes me a minority. But then again, we *control* the media!'

There's a huge laugh. I delivered the line perfectly! What a wonderful moment! I grin. OK! What's next?

For an hour an impassioned debate on racism ensues, punctuated by me sporadically muttering, in a strangled and panicky voice, 'Does anyone else on the panel have anything to say about this matter?'

It has been downhill for me since the opening joke. I'd spent so long in the run up to the debate luxuriating in its brilliance, I had no idea what to say next. This became clear to the audience when I introduced the panel and realized I had no idea what their names were. I had to fumble apologetically with sheaves of paper.

Now, one panellist – Shahid Malik MP – says we should spare a thought for disenfranchised white people suffering an identity crisis in these multicultural times.

'Yes!' I yell. Everyone looks up. Finally, the silent chairperson has something to say. What will it be?

'Working-class white people in Britain do have an inferiority complex,' I say. 'Whereas I was just in Paris, and in Paris the white people are proud to be Parisian. Why can't we white British people be more like white Parisians? Anyway I just wanted to make that observation.'

I fall silent again and look suicidal. The audience glare at me askance.

'I was only saying what Shahid said,' I hear myself shriek.

26 February 2007

For a while now, our cat Monty has been behaving in a paranoid fashion, staring out of the window at the front yard, his hairs prickling.

'He does seem upset,' says my wife, Elaine.

'Mmm?' I say. I'm playing with my new mobile phone. It has a video function. I film Monty looking paranoid and I play it back.

'Wow!' I say.

Monty goes outside and crouches fearfully in a corner. And then we see what's making him so scared. A large new vicious-looking cat is glaring at him from the pavement, ready to attack.

'Try and keep them apart until I get back,' I say.

I go inside and type 'cat' 'fight' 'help' into Google. The response comes: 'When you see two cats fighting, one thing you might do is to pour some cold water over them. A good soaking will usually break up the fight.' I fill Joel's water pistol with water and take it outside to Elaine.

She begins to squirt.

'Hang on,' I say. I turn on the video function and film the squirting.

'Ha!' I say, amazed at the quality of the film I am taking. 'Elaine, this is brilliant!'

Elaine continues to squirt. The vicious cat holds its ground. I take a close-up.

'Ha ha!' I say. 'Got it!'

At this moment, an elderly woman walking her dog passes. She slows her pace, and stares in palpable horror at the events unfolding before her eyes – Elaine squirting a cat with water and me filming it on my mobile phone whilst shrieking with apparent joy. She clearly thinks she is witnessing some sick, anti-feline happy-slapping. I want to tell her that it is a terrible mistake, it isn't what it seems, but then I realize that it is, in fact, exactly what it seems.

28 February 2007

About five years ago I was invited to be an arts pundit on the BBC programme *Newsnight Review*.

'Can I just say,' I told my fellow pundit Germaine Greer in the green room, 'that I'm an enormous admirer of your work.'

'Thank you,' said Germaine Greer.

She's *lovely*! I thought.

Then we were bustled into the studio and, suddenly, I was on live television. 'So, Jon Ronson,' said the presenter. 'What did you think of Joel Schumacher's new film, *Tigerland*?'

'Well . . . !' I began.

But then I stopped. I could sense I was being intensely stared at by Germaine Greer. She had positioned herself – just off camera – in my peripheral vision, and her eyes were bearing down on me. There seemed something odd about her stare and so I involuntarily glanced over at her to get a proper look. Her finger was pressed burlesquely against her cheek. Her mouth was silently frozen in the shape of an 'Ooooh!' as in 'Ooooh! How *interesting*! *Do* tell!' Hers was a face distorted into a mask of comic mock-fascination.

Germaine Greer is subtly trying to sabotage my performance! I thought, shocked. That's a bolt from the blue. Why would Germaine Greer want to put off a fledgling young arts pundit? Hasn't she got enough? She's Germaine Greer!

As a result I stumbled on live television, I saw Germaine Greer smile to herself with satisfaction – like a grand lioness seeing off a virile but naive young rival – and I was never invited back.

The incident sent a chill through me. Are we, as humans, never truly satisfied with what we have, I thought, and does this feeling of discontent only grow with age? I'm never going to be that way! Never!

It is five years later. I'm walking into town when I bump into Andrew, a journalist I knew years ago. 'You're doing well,' Andrew says. 'I see your name about.'

'Well, I wrote a conspiracy book that was better than *The Da Vinci Code* but didn't sell anywhere nearly as well,' I reply.

'Oh,' says Andrew. 'By the way, they've found flesh hanging from the railings in the park over there.' I glance over and see scores of police officers.

'Huh!' I say. There's something I want to add about my book's sales figures, but decide it would probably be appropriate to wait a moment.

'Human flesh?' I ask.

Andrew shrugs. 'There seems to have been some kind of ritual sacrifice,' he says.

'Huh!' I say again. 'Anyway. Don't get me wrong. My book *was* a success. Anyway, bye.'

'Bye,' says Andrew.

1 March 2007

I'm in an optician's, trying on a pair of sunglasses. The optician sidles up to me.

'Those sunglasses,' she says, 'were hand-crafted by jewellers during the Depression.'

'Oh, *really*?' I say, intrigued.

An image pops into my head of Depression-era jewellers painstakingly crafting sunglasses whilst hiding from the Nazis in attics. I wonder why every mental picture I have of twentieth-century history – regardless of continent or decade – includes the spectre of encroaching Nazis.

'I'll *take* them!' I say. 'Can I have prescription lenses put in, please?'

The optician says they'll take about a week. As I cycle home on my new folding Mezzo bike I think profound thoughts about the passing of time – how people are born and people die, how decades tumble inexorably by, but one thing remained constant throughout it all: my new sunglasses.

And they'll survive me too, I think, and end up on the face of someone in the future! Someone who hasn't even been *born* yet!

I cycle past a toddler and his posh-looking mother. 'Funny bike!' the toddler yells, pointing at me. I smile benevolently.

'Yes,' says the mother. 'Stupid bike.'

Huh? I think.

I stare at her open-mouthed as I cycle past.

The truth is, as a parent of a former toddler, I understand why she unexpectedly blurted out that insult. When you're raising a toddler – if you're crap at it and out of your depth – the rest of the world becomes nothing more than props, collateral damage in your pitiable attempts to enchant or even converse with it. I probably did it too. I probably left a trail of hurt feelings in my wake back then too.

'Yes, Joel,' I probably yelled. 'That child *is* fat. They *do* live in a tiny flat,' and so on. I shiver to think of it. The fact is, I now realize, raising a toddler is a walk in the park (literally, when you take them to the park) in comparison to – say – the hardships Depression-era jewellers must have suffered. I'm glad that these days I manage to keep things in perspective.

7 March 2007

The optician telephones.

'The lenses are all done,' she says, 'but unfortunately a little thing snapped on the frame when we were doing some adjustments, so we're just waiting for a replacement.'

'No problem!' I say.

14 March 2007

The optician calls.

'You sunglasses are completely ready!' she says.

'That's wonderful!' I say. 'I'll cycle over immediately and pick them up!'

I do. 'Here they are!' she says, pulling them out of a box.

'They're great!' I say.

'Brand-new lenses and brand-new frames!' she says.

There's a silence. I furrow my brow. 'Thank you,' I say, in a small voice.

I take the sunglasses home. I sit in my office, staring mistrustfully at them. After a while, Elaine comes home.

'So let's see them!' she says.

I put them on. 'They're *really nice*,' she says. 'Those old jewellers were really good.'

I fall silent.

'What?' Elaine says.

'Nothing,' I say.

I know what'll happen if I recount what occurred at the optician's to Elaine. She'll blow it up into a big crisis and make it all seem like it was my fault. No, I decide. It is best to keep silent. I'll keep my suspicions to myself.

'What?' Elaine sternly repeats.

I take a breath.

'Well,' I begin, 'when I picked them up from the optician's she said they had "brand-new lenses and brand-new frames". So now I'm thinking that if *every-thing* about them is brand new then they can no longer possibly be considered to be sunglasses that were made by Depression-era jewellers.'

There's a silence.

'It's fraud!' says Elaine. 'We're phoning them up right now.'

'Hang on, hang on,' I say, pacing the room. 'Calm down. Fraud is a *very* big word.'

'OK,' says Elaine. 'Let's go back to the beginning. When you picked them up, and she said that thing about the frames being new, what did you say?'

'Nothing,' I say.

'Why not?' says Elaine.

'Because I don't know what constitutes acceptable sunglasses in this scenario!' I yell. 'I was out of my depth. *OK?*'

It's true. When I think about it, I was out of my depth from the moment I entered the shop. This was a very posh optician's. When I tried them on she gave me an admiring look that was meant to convey, 'Some people don't deserve to wear sunglasses that were hand-crafted long ago by jewellers in distressed circumstances. Only the very finest gentlemen deserve that! And I know you are top notch, both in terms of handsomeness of face and successfulness of career.'

(It's interesting – thinking back – that she'd choose to emphasize the suffering the jewellers endured as a selling point. Corporations these days tend to underplay that kind of thing, by not letting journalists into their sweatshops, et cetera. I suppose suffering that took place seventy years ago seems quite exciting.)

Her admiring gaze wrong-footed me and filled me with false pride.

I *do* deserve the glasses, I thought, for all the reasons that your look just conveyed.

The truth is, I didn't want to blow all that mutual respect by getting into a big fight with her.

'And anyway,' I say to Elaine, '*I* was the one who wanted prescription lenses. So surely I'm fifty per cent to blame for the newness of the sunglasses. Had new frames gone around the original lenses, they'd still be considered authentic Depression-era sunglasses, right?' I pause. 'Or *would* they?' I say.

I'm reminded of the ancient conundrum. If I chop off my arm, I say, 'This is me and this is my arm.' But if I chop off my head, do I say, 'This is me and this is my head,' or 'This is me and this is my body?' What is the essence of being? Where does the soul of the sunglasses reside? If any original part remains – even the tiniest screw – are they not still, philosophically speaking, Depression-era sunglasses?

I explain all this to Elaine. She says, 'Will you just bloody phone them and demand a discount!'

'A retrospective discount?' I say, a pleading look in

my eyes. 'It's hard enough asking for a discount at the time.'

And then, suddenly, an extraordinary thought pops into my head.

'Elaine,' I say. 'Can we not just allow ourselves to *believe* that they were hand-crafted by Depression-era jewellers?'

'But . . .' says Elaine.

Then she goes quiet.

Tonight, we have friends round. I show them my sunglasses.

'They were hand-crafted by jewellers during the Depression,' says Elaine.

'Imagine that!' I say.

Elaine and I share a glance.

I think we're becoming more mature.

5 April 2007

Joel has been invited to audition for a local Sunday-morning theatre school. Their selection process is notoriously stringent, but I'm not worried. I know they'll just love him because he's so great.

'You'll *walk* it!' I say proudly as I drop him off.

Joel smiles unsurely. 'Good luck!' I call after him.
Like he needs it! I think.

Two hours pass. 'So?' I ask the theatre director.
'How was he?'

'Joel was a little distracted and he didn't listen,' he
replies. 'We take concentration very seriously. So we
don't know whether to accept him. We'll let you
know.'

We drive in silence back to the house.

Joel let himself down, I think, shooting him a dis-
appointed glance. Why would he do that? Why?

Back home, I tell Elaine the story. She looks sadly
out of the window. Then she turns to me.

'It isn't fair to blame Joel,' she says, 'when in fact
it's your fault.'

'Huh?' I say.

'You've been far too lenient and indulgent with
Joel all these years,' says Elaine.

'I have not,' I say.

But I know she's right. 'Well, that's it,' I say, 'I'm
not going to be lenient any more.'

I storm into the living room. Unfortunately Joel is
not doing anything that warrants non-leniency. He's
just watching TV. I sit there for a while, waiting for
him to put a foot wrong. But he doesn't. He just
watches TV. It is frustrating.

The next day, we fly to Scotland to spend a few days with Elaine's family in a country cottage. The mood on the journey is sombre. We haven't yet heard from the theatre school. Plus, much to Joel's bafflement, I have become unexpectedly strict, which is creating a weird atmosphere.

'Can I have one last biscuit?' says Joel on the plane.

'No, you cannot!' I unpredictably yell.

We stop off at Elaine's mother's house in Cumbernauld, near Glasgow, where we've arranged to meet up with six members of her family. Nine of us gather in Elaine's mother's kitchen.

'I'm just going to pop off to Asda to buy some All-Bran,' I say. 'I won't be five minutes.'

'I've got All-Bran here,' says Elaine's mother.

'Thanks very much indeed, Gran,' I say, 'but, honestly, I'll buy my own.'

There is a silence. Elaine, her mother, her brother, his wife and their children all look quizzically at me.

'Take my mum's All-Bran,' says Elaine.

I shoot Elaine a look to say, 'I have a reason for wanting my own All-Bran. Just trust me on this and let it go.'

But Elaine is in no mood to trust me. Something happens to her when she visits Scotland. She starts to see me in a whole different way, as some kind of fey

English invader, like the evil, lisping Prince Edward in *Braveheart*. She clearly suspects that my desire to have my own personal stash of brand-new All-Bran comes from the same well of southern, middle-class weakness that has led me to be too lenient with Joel all these years, hence our current problems with the theatre school.

'What's wrong with Gran's All-Bran?' says Elaine. 'Take Gran's All-Bran.'

'*I don't want Gran's All-Bran*,' I hiss.

'It's right here!' says Elaine's mother, pulling it out of the cupboard. She tries to thrust it into my hands. I flinch anxiously away from it.

'What's your problem with my mother's All-Bran?' asks Elaine.

'Yes,' says Elaine's mother. 'What?'

The others stare at me, their heads cocked.

I sigh. 'Because the last time I was here, I tried Gran's All-Bran, and it was stale, and that was three months ago, and I can tell that it's the same packet,' I say.

There's a silence.

'Will we go to the cottage, then?' says Elaine, brightly.

We set off. On the way, the theatre school telephones to say they'd be delighted to offer Joel a place.

It turns out that we'd been worrying about nothing.

9 April 2007

Monday evening. I'm with my wife's family in a country cottage in Scotland.

'Tomorrow,' I say, 'let's all rent pedalos and explore the loch!'

I picture the nine of us in pedalo convoy, mid-loch, exploring crannies, et cetera. That *does* seem like fun, I think.

The radio news is on. The forecast is for a sunny day.

'Maybe we should do the Highland Safari instead,' says Gran Paterson.

'No, pedalos will be *great*,' I say. I pause and add, 'Pedalos.'

'Ah!' says Elaine's brother, Frank. 'You should check the BBC online forecast too, because the radio didn't mention the wind direction. Check the wind direction.'

'Who checks wind direction?' I say, exasperated. 'Nobody!'

'Check the wind direction,' says Frank.

The mood has turned tense. I sigh, log onto the BBC weather page and make a big show of moving my eyes across the screen, to the weird stuff to the right of the sun symbol.

'Would you like to know the sun index too?' I say, my voice laden with heavy sarcasm.

'Just the wind direction,' says Frank.

'Moderate north-easterly,' I say.

'Ah ha!' says Frank. 'Then we can't do pedalos. It'll be too cold.'

Frank and I look at each other. 'Let's decide in the morning,' says Elaine.

10 April 2007

We're driving in convoy to Loch Tay. I'm in the car behind.

I'm so glad I've cured myself of all those crazy thoughts I used to have, I think as I drive. Hang on. Why is Frank zooming ahead like that? Does he not respect the concept of the convoy?

I put my foot on the accelerator. 'Slow down!' yells Elaine.

'It's your brother's fault!' I yell, screeching around a corner. 'I'm just trying to keep the convoy intact.'

'Forget the convoy!' yells Elaine.

We reach the loch. 'Pedalos!' I say.

'Not with a north-easterly wind,' says Frank. 'You can count me out.'

'There's no wind at all!' I say.

'There will be on the loch,' says Frank.

'Well, I'll go alone,' I mutter.

And I do. It is freezing out there, and very choppy. Nonetheless, I stay out for the full hour.

16 April 2007

It was Christmas Eve, sixteen years ago. I was twenty-three and writing a weekly column for *Time Out* magazine. That day my plan had been to finish the column fast, fax it off, do some quick last-minute Christmas shopping and get the evening train to my parents' house in Cardiff. The clock was ticking. The column was about Christmas shopping being annoying.

I'm making some pithy yet amusingly cruel observations! I thought as I feverishly typed. Finished! OK.

If I rush to the fax shop, fax it off and then hurry to Selfridge's, I might just make the 6 p.m. train. But first I must count the words.

I pulled the paper out of the typewriter and hurriedly counted. '573, 574, 575 . . . No!' I was twenty-five words short.

Damn! I thought. Quick, Jon. You just need one final observation about Christmas shopping being annoying. *Think!*

And then it came to me: 'If I hear that Paul McCartney Rupert Bear and the Frog Chorus song coming out of a tannoy one more time,' I wrote, 'I'm going to open fire. Mark Chapman truly shot the wrong Beatle.'

I paused and looked at the page. That'll do, I thought.

Two weeks later I opened the post to discover a letter from Linda McCartney. 'So are you saying that you hope my husband – and the father of my children – is killed in cold blood by the man who murdered his best friend?' she wrote.

I stared at the letter. I'm going to pretend I never received this, I thought. I'm just going to put it in a drawer and carry on as if nothing had happened.

But, really, I knew she was right. Viciously insulting people in print for no good reason was no way to live one's life. And so, as a result of that letter, I stopped doing it.

It is sixteen years later and Jimmy Wales – the founder of Wikipedia – has come to believe that blogs are bringing out the worst in people. He's consequently backed a 'code of conduct' that he hopes bloggers will henceforth adhere to, including: 'We will not post unacceptable content used to abuse, harass, stalk, or threaten others.'

I stare at the Google Blogs search box after I read this.

Dare I? I think. Dare I type my own name into it? How bad can it be? I cannot stop myself. I feel beckoned into the unknown. I type my name and I press search.

Three hours later I stumble out of my office a paranoid, empty husk. My eyes dart up and down the street. I'm now mistrustful of everyone. Looking yourself up on Google truly is (in the words of *The Thick Of It*) like opening the door to a room where everybody thinks you're shit. One woman cannot bear to think that I live within a few miles of her. Perhaps one day she'll see me in the flesh and vomit all over me. Another 'potently hates' me. And so on. Who are these people? How did blogging get so vicious?

I think I have the answer: the Internet gives us the

illusion that we're wonderfully gregarious people. When we type away on discussion boards and post comments on one another's blogs it feels like we're sitting outside a pub in the evening sunshine with our attractive, cool friends. But we aren't. That's something we used to do before we got addicted to the Internet. What we do instead is perform some empty, unsatisfying facsimile of that. We sit alone in our rooms, becoming more and more isolated from society. And, inevitably, this turns us into mad, yelling, wild-eyed loons.

Thank God looking oneself up on Google is a secret vice, I think. Thank God the people who hate me don't know that I've been reading their blogs. That would be mortifying.

Three days pass. Then I look myself up on Google again.

'Jon Ronson is *so* self-absorbed,' someone writes. 'I just looked at my webstats and found a visitor from ronson.demon.co.uk. The simpering twat looked himself up!'

They somehow *knew*! I think. What the hell are webstats?

There is only one thing for it. I'm going to write them stern Linda McCartney-style letters, telling them off for insulting me.

The only way to preserve my dignity, I think, is to be like Linda McCartney.

19 April 2007

It is six months ago. I'm sitting in a Starbucks toilet in Stockport when my Palm Pilot rings. It is my great socialist friend Michael.

'What are you up to?' he asks me.

'I'm in Stockport,' I reply.

I don't mention that I'm in a toilet because one doesn't just yell out, 'I'm sitting on a toilet!' What kind of person would do that? Not the sort of person I'd want as a friend.

No, I think. I'll keep the fact that I'm on the toilet a secret from Michael.

'I'm back in London tomorrow,' I say. 'I'll be taking Joel for skateboarding lessons.'

'*Skateboarding* lessons!' he scoffs. 'You're so middle class!'

Yeah yeah, I think. Everything's always class class class with you.

There's someone outside the cubicle. I can hear them shuffle around. They, in turn, can hear me talking in here.

I hope they realize I'm talking on the phone and don't think I'm doing some kind of drug deal or having sex in here with someone, I think. Of course when I come out alone they'll know, but perhaps I should adopt an 'I'm on the phone being normal and not doing anything sordid' tone of voice, loud enough to be heard through the door, just to clarify things now. Yes, that's what I'll do.

I'm about to, when I'm confronted with another more pressing problem: I've finished the toilet and I need to flush. But how can I without Michael hearing it? Michael is chatting obliviously away about socialism and so it would be rude to cut him short just so I can hang up and flush the toilet with impunity. Yet it would be equally rude to keep the person outside waiting until Michael finishes whatever it is he's telling me about socialism. That person is probably desperate for the toilet.

Ah ha! I think. I'll kill two birds with one stone! I'll start talking loudly, in a chatty way, so the person outside will know I'm not having sex or taking drugs, and I'll simultaneously flush the toilet, which Michael won't hear because of my effusive chatter. Now I just have to bide my time until the perfect moment.

'. . . the means of production,' says Michael.

'I don't necessarily believe that skateboarding

lessons are middle class,' I spiritedly yell. I flush the toilet. 'They have to learn somehow,' I screech. I simultaneously jerk my Palm Pilot downwards, in the hope that the whooshing motion of the phone will create a wind effect that will further camouflage the flushing sound.

It is at this moment that the Palm Pilot slips out of my hand and lands in the toilet.

No! I think. NOOOOO!

I stare down wretchedly at the Palm Pilot, lying at the base of the bowl.

The terrible irony is that Michael, being a socialist, probably wouldn't have minded at all that I was conversing with him whilst sitting on the toilet. Socialists don't care about that kind of thing. Only the bourgeois care. If I've learnt anything from Luis Buñuel I've learnt that.

Maybe it can be saved! I think. They're built sturdily these days.

I reach in and grab it. It sits lifelessly on my palm.

Oh dear, I think.

And then, horrifically, it splutters to a kind of bizarre, mutant form of life. It starts vibrating in a way it has never vibrated before, like a grotesque, dying wasp. I recoil in disgust and fear. It is like that scene in *Fatal Attraction* when the drowned Glenn

Close suddenly jerks back to life for one final, shocking moment. It is like a zombie phone. It might electrocute me. I chuck it in the bin.

I know, I think. I'll buy myself a BlackBerry. I've been wanting to for a while.

I first became aware of the BlackBerry the night I went to see *Stomp*, a musical about how crusties are better than the rest of us because they can discern beauty in dustbins whereas all we can do is throw our garbage into them like greedy bourgeois pigs. The man in front of me spent half the show frantically sending and receiving emails on his BlackBerry. It lit up his face in the dark like an alluringly golden jewel.

Wow! I thought. If that's an addiction, I want to get addicted!

Maybe dropping my Palm Pilot down the toilet will turn out to be the best thing that's every happened to me.

21 April 2007

My BlackBerry arrives.

Who will I email first? I wonder. It seems appropriate to choose Michael. 'Would you like to have a drink tonight?' I write. I press send.

'Oh WAS it now?' Michael instantly emails back.

Strange, I think. I telephone Michael.

'I'm sorry about that,' he explains. 'When I read your email I thought *you'd* written at the bottom "Sent from my BlackBerry Wireless Handheld", but now I realize it was an auto-signature.'

'An auto-signature?' I say.

'BlackBerry has pre-programmed your phone to let everyone you email know that you're doing it from a BlackBerry,' says Michael. 'Just another sick corporate trick.'

'Yeah,' I say. 'Corporate pigs, forcing me to be a walking billboard for them. Well, I'm phoning customer services right now to tell them to disable it.'

I hang up, begin dialling customer services, and then stop. I look guiltily around the room. Then I put the phone down. The fact is, I like having the auto-signature. I like people knowing my email was sent from my BlackBerry wireless device.

My recipients will presumably read the message and think, If he's emailing from a BlackBerry he must be *out*. I wonder where? Probably somewhere interesting. What a life that man has! What a *life*!

And best of all, it isn't me that's boasting. It is the auto-signature. I don't have to do *anything*. It's like having someone run around behind me saying complimentary things about me to everyone, while I just blush demurely and make out as if I wish they'd stop. I am Marlon Brando in *Apocalypse Now*, and my auto-signature is Dennis Hopper, yelling, 'I'm a little man! He's a *great* man!'

24 April 2007

On Tuesday, I'm having a bad day. I'm stuck at home and I can't think of anything to write. I stare glumly out of the window. Then I receive an email from an ex-girlfriend called Deborah. She was my first love. She dumped me fifteen years ago for a man called Jack.

'We've not spoken in ages!' Deborah writes. 'What are you up to?'

'Actually I'm having a bit of a crap day . . .' I begin to reply. And then I stop. I stare at my BlackBerry, sitting on my desk.

Oh, why not? I think.

'Everything's great,' I type. 'How are you? Sent from my BlackBerry Wireless Handheld.'

'Not so good,' Deborah writes back. 'Jack's been made redundant again. We don't have any money. The other day I was in a toyshop and I accidentally walked out holding a *Thomas the Tank Engine* book that I hadn't paid for. I was on the street when I realized what I'd done. So I turned to go back into the shop. But do you know what I did instead? I carried on walking.'

'That's terrible,' I reply. 'I'm so sorry. Sent from my BlackBerry Wireless Handheld.'

'I'm a thirty-seven-year-old shoplifter,' writes Deborah. 'That's what my life is.'

'Don't blame yourself,' I type. 'Sent from my BlackBerry Wireless Handheld.'

28 April 2007

I'm cycling along the canal. A couple of walkers in front of me stray into my path. I swerve frantically to avoid them.

Bloody pedestrians, I think. They don't even *think* about us cyclists.

Then I hear the ping of my BlackBerry, telling me I have an email.

An *email*! I think, excitedly.

I still find it exciting to receive emails. And texts. Messages on my telephone answering-machine at home, less so. I don't even bother listening to them half the

time. That flashing red light can flash away for days –
I just don't care. But when I hear the ping of an
incoming email, I'll instantly stop whatever I'm doing
to read it. It's quite irrational, really. I'll jump off
bikes. I'll rush upstairs. I've developed a fail-safe
method of reading them undetected whilst in conversation with my wife in a restaurant. Elaine will be in
the middle of saying something, I'll hear the ping,
continue to nod and smile exactly as I was before the
ping, surreptitiously pull the BlackBerry out of my
pocket, rest it on my lap, keep looking into Elaine's
eyes, wait for her to say the kind of important thing
that would require me to bow my head as if deep in
thought, and then quickly read the email.

Why are emails so much more exciting to receive
than telephone answering-machine messages? It's
probably the ping. It sounds like a magical genie has
unexpectedly appeared and is ready to grant wishes. I
hear that ping now as I cycle along the canal. I screech
to a halt and dismount. A cyclist tears past me.

Bloody cyclists, I think. They don't even *think*
about us pedestrians.

It is a round-robin email from a work colleague:
'Just to let you know that I'll be away for the next 10
days,' she writes. 'My grandfather has died unexpec-

tedly aged 86. We are all very shocked about it. So I'm taking time off to be with the family.'

Well, he had a good innings, I think. I wonder if I should email back offering my condolences and pointing out that he had a good innings?

I pause and furrow my brow. Should I? I think. If I point out that he had a good innings, will she read it as, 'Oh, come on! It's hardly *untimely*. It's timely! Let's not get self-indulgent! The seeming depth of your grief is not justified.' On the other hand, perhaps a reminder of the length of his innings will help them get over their shock. What to do, what to do?

I'm bad at offering condolences. I've never worked out how to do it. I think you can bluff your way through life, feigning utter competence in all circumstances, right up until the moment you're compelled to offer condolences. I think the worst thing I ever said to anyone was a bungled condolence. A great friend of mine once told me her mother had just died of septicaemia. I replied, '*Everyone's* dying of septicaemia! I know three people who died of septicaemia in two weeks. What the hell is going on with septicaemia?'

I think that moment will pop into my head on my deathbed and I will die blushing. Or maybe it wasn't too bad a thing to say. I just don't know.

I am going to mention the innings in my condolence email, I think now. And so I write back, 'I'm so sorry to hear about your grandfather. 86 though. Wow! Am thinking of you. Jon. Sent from my BlackBerry Wireless Handheld.'

I cycle home. As I do, my phone bounces around in my pocket, resending my condolence email over and over. By the time I reach home I have offered her my condolences forty-three times.

And so the death of a loved one will once again be inextricably linked in the mind of the bereaved with my inefficient offering of condolence, I think, ruefully. Should I email her a forty-fourth time to explain that it was a telephone malfunction and not a psychotic meltdown? I wonder. I decide to let it lie.

2. THINKING INSIDE THE BOX

A young man called Bill stands in the shadows behind a curtain at a converted paintworks factory in Bristol, now a TV studio.

'To be honest,' Bill says, 'I'm a little bit shell-shocked.'

'This is it!' yells a man called Jim. 'Concentrate, Bill! Hit it! Hit it! Hit it! Let's do it, mate! Come on! Come on!'

'I'm bricking it,' says Bill.

'Go out there!' Jim says. 'Fierce! Do it! Be affirmative, man! Win some money! Do it! Positive! THIS IS YOUR MOMENT! THIS IS YOUR CHANCE! GO! GO! GO! GO! GO!'

And at that, Bill steps out from the shadows to rapturous applause, and he proceeds randomly to open the first of twenty-two boxes.

Nine months ago I was on a treadmill at the gym. A Channel 4 afternoon game show called *Deal or No*

Deal was on the TV. I'd never seen it before so it took me a minute to understand what was going on.

Twenty-two contestants stood behind twenty-two boxes. One of them, Fin, was selected to be that day's player. There was a cash prize inside each box, from 1p to £250,000. Each time a box was opened, whatever cash prize was in there was discounted. Fin would win whatever money was left in the last box he opened. From time to time a telephone rang and a mysterious person on the other end, the Banker, tried to tempt Fin to stop opening the boxes by offering him a cash settlement. And that was it. That was the game.

It's all luck, I thought. It's a game show with no skill. He's just opening boxes. What a terrible idea.

Forty-five minutes later I was convinced that *Deal Or No Deal* was the greatest game show I'd ever seen, full of unbearable drama and unexpected weirdness.

At first, Fin looked pretty ordinary. But then he produced a scrap of paper from his pocket and showed it to presenter Noel Edmonds.

'It contains distilled wisdom from Paulo Coelho's *The Alchemist*,' he said.

'I like the sound of this, Fin,' Noel replied. 'You've got a sensitive, almost spiritual side.'

How does Fin think distilled wisdom from Paulo Coelho's *The Alchemist* will help him choose the right boxes? I thought as I jogged. It's all luck. And when did Noel Edmonds suddenly get so mystical?

There was a close-up of the scrap of paper, upon which Fin had scribbled 'Listen to your heart.'

Suddenly a trancelike state overwhelmed Fin as he scanned the boxes.

'What's going through your mind?' Noel asked.

'I'm trying to just let the numbers come to me,' Fin said.

'For a big guy you're looking incredibly serene,' said Noel.

'I'm listening to my heart,' Fin said. 'Box number sixteen, please.'

It was opened. £5 was in there. The audience cheered. Now, Fin wouldn't go home with the paltry sum of £5.

And so it continued. Fin's psychic trance state turned out to be an astonishing triumph. He opened the £1 box, the 50p box and the 10p box. Noel and the audience and I watched awed, as if witnessing a miracle.

'The way you're playing the game is actually more powerful than luck itself!' Noel said.

It was turning into one of the most exciting television-viewing experiences I'd ever had. Each time a box was opened the tension was so agonizing I was practically running a four-minute mile on the treadmill. Although this was quarter past four in the afternoon, four million viewers – nearly half of everyone watching TV at that moment – were watching Fin.

Then the banker phoned and offered Fin a huge cash settlement of £44,000. The audience gasped. A mystical look crossed Fin's face.

'No deal!' he said. There was cheering.

And then disaster struck. Fin opened the £100,000 box, followed, devastatingly, by the £250,000 box. He ended up walking away with a relatively crappy £10,000.

Everybody in the audience – including Noel – went quiet and looked embarrassed and even a little ashamed. The mood was what I imagined it must feel like when somebody turns on all the lights at an orgy. The fact is, Fin should have accepted the £44,000. Listening to his heart and making decisions based on psychic impulses cost him £34,000. It was a victory for rational and vaguely negative thinking.

My God, I thought, as I finally climbed off the treadmill, exhausted. They're in a bubble. They've got no sense of reality. They have, in Noel Edmonds, a charismatic leader who believes in nutty things. It's like a religious cult! An incredibly nail-biting and entertaining cult, but a cult nonetheless.

And so I phoned Endemol, the show's producers. I asked if I could be a fly on their wall. The show is filmed in Bristol, they said. The first anniversary show would be filmed in early October. I was welcome to come along.

And so now it is early October, in Bristol, and despite all the backstage motivational pumping by Jim the Contestant Carer, Bill is having a terrible game. He's randomly opening all the wrong boxes. They film three shows a day here, and this is the last. It is especially awful to watch because this morning another contestant, Dan, won £70,000.

I'm sitting in the green room next to Pete the coach driver. Pete ferries the contestants between the hotel and the studio. His contact with them is minimal. This morning Pete announced to the coach that he'd be grateful if people stopped calling him Driver.

'I hate that,' Pete said. 'My name is Pete.'

Now, as we watch Bill's painful show unfold on the monitor screen, I can hear Pete whisper to himself. I listen closer. He's murmuring, 'Come on, Bill. Believe. Keep the dream alive.'

But it doesn't work out. Bill opens the wrong boxes

to the end and walks away with a devastating £750. He emerges from the studio drained of colour. We climb onto the coach. Pete drives us back to the hotel in silence.

Deal Or No Deal was invented within Endemol's Dutch HQ. It has sold to forty-five countries, from Albania to Vietnam. When Endemol developed the format for British television, they came up with a brilliant idea. In other countries, such as the USA, the people standing behind the boxes, the box-openers, are professional models, former *Playboy* centrefolds, et cetera. They all wear identical showgirl costumes. UK Endemol's brilliant idea was to make the box-openers fellow contestants – players-to-be. This means they're all sequestered away together at a hotel in Bristol, sometimes for weeks on end, away from the anchor of their homes, while they await their chance to get out from behind the boxes and become the main player. Consequently, an intense group bond forms. Late at night in the hotel tiny things become huge things. Emotions are heightened. And in the morning, when filming begins, you can feel the drama in the winces and the cheers and the looks of love and hate that pass between the contestants.

*

According to the Cult Information Centre's pamphlet, *Cults: A Practical Guide*, cult leaders routinely employ twenty-six skilful techniques to keep their followers under their spell. One of the main ones is 'Isolation: inducing loss of reality by physical separation from family, friends, society and rational references.' Endemol – who make *Big Brother* as well as *Deal or No Deal* – realize that isolation doesn't only produce good cults, it also produces good television.

Now, as the coach trundles miserably back to the hotel, I realize this is the first time that the mood has been at anything less than a fever pitch of positivity. Jim the Contestant Carer is forever giving the contestants motivational talks. We're getting about four every day.

'GROUP CHEER!' Jim constantly yells, his eyes aflame.

I wonder if this is in any way because of Noel Edmonds' famous antipathy towards negativity. In fact Noel writes in his recently published self-help book, *Positively Happy*, that he can't abide negativity in the workplace. Noel hates negativity. In fact he hates negativity so much, I would suggest his antipathy towards it borders on the negative. He even advises readers, on page 88, to dump their sexual partners if they are too negative. I can't help thinking that if I were Noel Edmonds' lover, he would dump me.

'But surely a bit of negativity makes you – you know – interestingly spiky and sassy,' I suggested to Noel earlier during a break from filming.

'I simply will not now get involved with people who are negative,' Noel replied. 'I won't tolerate people in the workplace who are negative. I like realistic people, but negative people? No. Just get rid of them.'

'I have a habit of being a bit negative sometimes,' I said. 'I'd hate my wife to read *Positively Happy* and dump me as a result.'

'Then be careful,' Noel said, looking me in the eye, 'because she might.'

There was a silence.

Actually, Kevin the studio warm-up man yesterday was a bit negative too. His job was to whip the audience into a frenzy of excitement. And Kevin did have an upbeat voice, but the things he said were terribly miserable.

'I'm so sad,' he told the audience yesterday, 'that if I went to a wife-swapping party where everyone throws their keys into the middle, I'd be the only one to walk home alone! That's how ugly I am!'

The audience shuffled uncomfortably in their seats. That was yesterday. Today, Kevin was nowhere to be seen. He's been replaced by a far more cheerful and upbeat warm-up man called Mark.

It is 10 p.m., back in the hotel. I have a drink with contestant Tony from the West Midlands. Earlier, during recording, Tony was standing behind box 8 and Noel mentioned that he thought he looked like a funeral director. It got a laugh: Tony does look slightly undertakerish, with white hair, a white moustache and a long, thin face. Now, unbeknownst to everyone else, Tony is desperately worried about it.

'I'm semi-retired,' he explains. 'Everything in my life revolves around quarter past four. I do the washing, the cleaning and I sit down. *Deal Or No Deal* is an addiction for me. So to actually get through the auditions and on to the show! I'm dreaming! Apparently the chances of becoming a contestant are seventy thousand to one. And I make it through all that, and Noel calls me a funeral director.' Tony pauses. 'If only he could see the real me. Maybe I should have laughed or something. But to stand there and laugh at nothing? It's hard. And I didn't sleep well last night. There were police cars going up and down all night. Was Noel aware of that?'

Suddenly, Tony stops and glances at my notepad.

'Where's this information going?' he asks. 'Is it going to the Banker?'

There's a lot of paranoia amongst the contestants that things they say and do in the hotel might be relayed to the Banker – the mysterious figure on the other end of the phone who is never seen or heard. They fear that when it's their turn to play, the Banker might give them low cash offers if they've been deemed to have behaved desperately or cowardly or negatively back at the hotel.

'It isn't going to the Banker,' I say.

Tony pauses.

'Are you giving it to someone who'll give it to the Banker?' he asks.

'No,' I say.

At this, Tony relaxes. And it is true: Noel hasn't seen the real him. He's a warm, lovely man. As we drink he keeps asking me, 'What can I do to make Noel realize that I'm nothing like a funeral director?'

Every night after dinner there's a contestants' meeting. It is a chance for the three main players of the day to dissect their games. Bill – the £750 winner – takes the floor.

'I just want to say,' he says, 'that the Banker was a

twat and a dickhead and thank God he wasn't standing in front of me.'

Bill sits down again.

'You stood strong, Bill,' says a contestant called
Edward. 'That's what matters. You stood strong.'

I glance over at Dan, today's £70,000 winner.
Ironically, Dan is probably the most secular person
here. He's always laughing to me about his fellow
contestants' crazy systems. And then he went and
won £70,000. There's a big smile on Dan's face now.
His beautiful girlfriend is draped over him. They
spent the afternoon shopping for designer clothes.
Then I glance back at Bill, looking hunched and
lonely. I resist the temptation to think that this was
somehow predestined by fate, that Dan looks a winner, and always did, and Bill looks a loser. But I don't
think that, because it is an entirely irrational thing to
think.

Then I am asked to take the floor to introduce myself.

'Some people apparently believe that I'm not really
from the *Guardian*,' I say, 'but am in fact the Banker's
spy! Well, I just want to say, I might be!'

I pause to receive laughter, but there isn't any.

'We're serious,' a few people say. 'Are you or aren't
you working for the Banker?'

'I'm not,' I say.

They give me three cheers.

Some contestants get drunk. The drinkers are, I've noticed, the secular ones who realize like I do that the box opening is all about luck and not at all spiritual. Maybe the weight of that knowledge is enough to drive you to the bottle. Other contestants sit quietly and concentrate on their systems.

Ned from Liverpool has a system. He shows it to me. It is a series of boxes and Xs, like some weird periodic table, printed on a neatly folded piece of A4 paper.

'What I did,' Ned explains, 'was discard the seventeen numbers that make up my name: NEIL THOMAS CULSHAW. So, for instance, the number 1 has gone because it corresponds with the letter A. So I'm left with five numbers, and I've put them in the order of which boxes contained the highest amounts during last week's shows. But I've *reversed* the order, based on the assumption that if they contained the highest amounts last week, they'll contain the lowest amounts for me. So bearing all that in mind, the five numbers I'm leaving to the end are 16, 17, 10, 22 and 18.'

'So you believe you've calculated that when you're the main player, box 18 will be the box most likely to contain £250,000?' I ask.

'Yes,' says Ned, confidently.

'Complex,' I say.

'Not really,' says Ned.

I'm surprised that so many contestants still put such stock in their systems. If the show has taught us anything over the past twelve months, it has taught us that systems don't work and people aren't telepathic. Contestant Steve has a lucky number but he won't tell me what it is in case sharing the information inadvertently robs the number of its power.

One day last week John – who claimed to be both telepathic *and* have a foolproof system – had his chance as the main player. John, a retired bank manager, had assiduously analysed a hundred and five shows. At night in the hotel he sat apart from the others, studying sheaves of spreadsheets. He concluded that boxes 1, 2, 5, 6, 18 and 19 were the luckiest. John's telepathy manifested itself in a tingle in his fingers. If he laid his fingers on a box, and his fingers tingled, he knew the box contained a high amount. John was convinced that his telepathy, coupled with his system, would make him unbeatable.

In the end, John walked away with £1.

*

Nonetheless, the contestants tonight are undaunted.

'John wasn't telepathic,' says contestant Nalini. 'But I've always been telepathic. One night I jumped out of bed. I said to my husband, "Something bad has happened." He said, "Don't be ridiculous." I said, "I mean it. I can't go to work because I know something terrible has happened." And later I discovered that this was the exact moment that my oldest son died. It was in the Maldives. That's the other side of the world. The exact moment. That was ten years ago.'

Still, Nalini says she doesn't want her turn as the main player to come just yet because that means she'd have to leave the bubble and go home.

'I love being here,' she says. 'My husband is a driver for Iceland, and on Saturdays he drinks.' Nalini shrugs. 'So I prefer being here in the hotel. This is a holiday.'

Then Nalini pauses and moves closer to me. 'Some people think too much,' she says. 'They go mad in the hotel.'

But for Bill, who just walked away with a terrible £750, there is no talk of systems or psychic powers any more. For him, the bubble is burst.

'I'm not worried any more that I lost,' he tells me. 'I'm worried about coming over as a twat on TV.'

'You didn't,' I say.

'If people say, "There's that twat," it'll make the rest of my life very hard,' Bill says.

I go to bed. In the middle of the night the fire alarm goes off twice. I have to traipse down nine flights of stairs to the car park.

The next morning, everyone is exhausted. I visit Noel in his Winnebago. It is parked up deep within the Endemol complex, near a dried-up river. Inside, it is very luxurious, all cream leather seats. Les Dennis's far smaller and less deluxe Winnebago is parked up next to it. Les Dennis is filming a Channel 5 game show called *Speculation* in another studio here.

'Les Dennis can have the big Winnebago when he gets the ratings we get,' says Noel.

I stealthily glance around the Winnebago for little clues that might reveal dark secrets of Noel's personal life. Noel's love life has been of interest ever since he made it known earlier this year that he asked the Cosmos to provide him with a woman.

Noel believes that if you order wishes from the Cosmos, the Cosmos will oblige, just as long as you follow the correct ordering protocols. You must write your wish down on a piece of paper. You absolutely have to be positive. The Cosmos will not accept negative wishes. You must keep your wish general. The Cosmos won't, for some reason, grant over-specific wishes.

As Noel explains the ins and outs of Cosmic Ordering to me I involuntarily look dubious. Immediately, Noel changes tack to insist he hasn't gone 'off with the fairies'.

'Yes, the word Cosmos might sound off-putting,' he says, 'but you don't have to call it Cosmos. Cosmos is just a word. You can call it anything you like. You can call it Argos or MFI.'

It strikes me that Noel Edmonds is probably the only modern-day spiritualist guru who would even consider Argos or MFI as alternative names for the Cosmos. That's the odd thing about hanging around here. The mystical people are not at all New Agey. They are retired bank managers. They work in betting shops. They are Noel Edmonds. The last time I saw Noel was ten years ago. He barged past me in some country house hotel towards his helicopter – the epitome of the no-nonsense Conservative businessman and celebrity, off to do some deal. He was nothing like the vulnerable, spiritual Noel sitting in front of me now.

'I wrote to the Cosmos that I would like to meet a

woman who'll make me laugh and make me happy,' Noel tells me. 'I wrote that I'd like a relationship that's not too heavy with an attractive lady, and I'd like her to walk into my life by the end of September 2005. And she did!'

There is a short silence.

'She wasn't the person who sold her story to the *Sunday People* back in July, was she?' I ask.

There's another silence.

'Yes,' says Noel.

He was a very tender and lovely kisser. When I woke up with him the following morning I felt completely at ease and his first words were, 'Cup of tea, darling?' He was a very giving man in all aspects and satisfied me in every way. Noel had his own special song for us. It was 'You're Beautiful' by James Blunt. But once he was back at the top he didn't need me any more. I felt he just discarded me. He was a hypocrite who used me to make himself feel more positive about himself.

– Marjan Simmons, the *Sunday People*, August 2006

'So that turned out to be not so good,' I say. 'Maybe if you'd written down, "I want to meet some-body by the end of September and I don't want her selling her story to the *Sunday People*—"'

'No, you can't do that,' Noel interrupts, 'because that's a negative. The Cosmos only accepts positive orders. The word I probably missed out was "trustworthy".'

I continue to peer surreptitiously around to see if I can spot anything weird or secret in the Winnebago. Noel almost immediately notices what I'm doing.

'Go and have a look in the bedroom,' he says. 'Go on.'

I look doubtfully at him. 'Are you sure?' I ask.

'Have a look in the bedroom,' he says.

I shoot Noel a slightly suspicious glance and then I wander into his bedroom. I have a good poke around. And unfortunately I find nothing incriminating. Still, it was nice of him to offer.

I tell Noel that I can't understand why he doesn't give up the mysticism. I've spent three days here, watching three shows a day, and I've seen so many disappointments, so many broken dreams, so many systems – telepathic or otherwise – that didn't pan out. And Noel has presented three hundred shows. By now he must know that life is just random.

Well first, Noel replies, it was the Cosmos that gave him *Deal Or No Deal*. The BBC had unceremoniously dumped him in 1999 after twenty years as a star presenter. It looked like he'd never be on TV again. He was a workaholic without work. So he spent five fallow years throwing himself into various businesses and charities – the British Horse Society, some anti-wind-farm lobby group called the Renewable Energy Foundation, et cetera. But he asked the Cosmos for a new work challenge, and the Cosmos gave him *Deal Or No Deal*. It was a huge and instant success, nominated for a Bafta, and winning a Royal Television Society Award and a Rose D'Or, all within a few months.

'Have you looked *Deal Or No Deal* up on the Internet?' Noel asks. 'It can do your head in. Did you know that someone's compiling a dictionary of my phrases?'

This is true. A large Wikipedia entry is dedicated to Noel's oft-repeated expressions ('Some people call it an entertainment drama, some the Red Box Club . . . Welcome to Planet Tension!' 'It's not how you start, it's how you finish.' And so on.)

'Somebody else,' says Noel, 'is tracking the repetition of my shoes, trousers and shirts.' Noel is thrilled: 'I'm delighted people are reading so much into it. I want to be popular. I want people to like me. Not long ago I talked to someone in the audience and she went to pieces. Just because I was talking to her! It is really important I keep my feet on the ground here.'

I don't think Noel should be thanking the Cosmos for the success of *Deal Or No Deal*. I think it takes a rare presenting talent to make the opening of twenty-two boxes so gripping.

But then Noel says there's something else. There's another reason why he still believes. He says that after three hundred shows he now knows – practically every time – how someone's going to do before they've opened a single box.

There's a silence.

'How?' I ask.

Noel pauses. 'How deep can I go here?' he says.

Then he says, 'Take Edward. Edward, I'm really not sure about. I've got a funny feeling it may go horribly wrong for Edward.'

Noel says he knows this just by the way Edward walks, his aura. You can tell winners by the way they walk. And Edward doesn't walk that way. Yesterday, one contestant, Mark, told me that Edward needed a big win more than anyone here: 'Edward's got nothing,' Mark said. 'Literally nothing. He's completely skint.'

I know something Edward doesn't know. I've seen the call sheet. Edward's game is going to start in a couple of hours.

Just before I leave the Winnebago, I spot a typed

sheet of paper lying on the kitchenette. I look closer. It contains notes about what the contestants got up to in the hotel last night.

'It started because of ill health,' Noel explains. 'Everyone was getting colds. I needed to know what was happening.'

But once the colds cleared up, the daily reports to Noel continued. For example, Noel says, if a pair of amorous contestants are seen leaving the bar together, a production assistant will write the news down and Noel will read about it at breakfast. He probably won't refer to it during the show, he says, but it is important for him to know what's going on. Today's sheet reads, 'Tony is very sensitive about your funeral-director comment.'

I leave Noel and wander back to the contestants. They're in make-up. Jim is giving them a motivational talk.

'The sun's out!' he says. 'It's a brand-new day! Let's really lift ourselves! Are we going to stick it right down the Banker's throat? Yeah? Yeah! Momentum! Get momentum! GROUP CHEER!'

Everyone cheers.

Tony is still worried about Noel's funeral-director aside. He says he telephoned his wife last night in a terrible flap about it.

'I said to her, "Rita? Am I miserable?" She said, "You're not." I said, "I love you forever." ' Tony pauses. 'But, Jon, you know what? I have a plan.'

He hands me a brown envelope. I open it to find a photograph of Tony's father standing next to Lester Piggott.

'Noel is President of the British Horse Society,' Tony explains. 'If I can get him to see this photograph ... Noel will know that a horse lover can't be miserable.'

Inside the make-up room, a contestant called Madeline is talking about last night's fire alarms.

'I had to walk down ten flights of stairs in my nightie,' she tells the make-up lady. Then she spots Jim the Motivational Carer.

'But you have to laugh, though, because it was really funny,' she quickly adds.

We walk into the studio. It is time for the contestants to choose their box numbers. This is done randomly: they reach in and grab ping-pong balls from a bag.

Contestant Nalini, who claims to be telepathic, turns to Contestant David and says, 'You're going to pick number seven.'

David reaches into the bag and pulls out ping-pong ball number 7.

Nalini smiles to herself. Everyone goes quiet.

Noel emerges from the wings and wanders up the line, saying hello to the contestants. He reaches Tony.

'How are you?' he says.

'HA! HA! HA! HA! HA!' says Tony, throwing his head back and letting out a huge, Santa Claus-type laugh. Then Tony spots me. He winks, as if to say, 'I *did* it!'

I give him a surreptitious thumbs-up.

And then the recording begins, and – as I knew he would be – Edward is picked. This is Edward who is penniless, Edward who needs it more than anyone, Edward who – Noel has psychically predicted – will have a terrible game, because he doesn't have the aura of a winner.

Two hours later, and the contestants are crying. Nalini blames it on the fire alarms.

'We're all so tired,' she says. 'If we haven't got the energy, how can we give off positive vibes? That's why Edward opened all the wrong boxes.'

Whatever: Noel was right. Edward walks away with just £1.

3. THE CHOSEN ONES

Eight-year-old Oliver Banks thinks he sees dead people. Recently he thought he saw a little girl with black hair climb over their garden fence in Harrow, Middlesex. Then – as he watched – she vanished. When Oliver was three he was at a friend's house, on top of the climbing frame, when he suddenly started yelling, 'Train!' He was pointing over the fence to the adjacent field. It turned out that, generations earlier, a railway line had passed through the field, exactly where he was pointing.

Oliver's mother, Simone, was at her wits' end. Last summer, at a party, she told her work colleagues about Oliver's symptoms. He wasn't concentrating at school. He couldn't sit still. Plus, he'd had a brain scan and they'd found all this unusual electrical activity. And then there were the visions of the people who weren't there. Maybe Oliver had attention deficit hyperactivity disorder?

At that moment, a woman standing nearby interrupted. She introduced herself as Dr Munchie. She said she couldn't help but eavesdrop on Simone's conversation. She was, she said, a qualified GP.

'Well, then,' Simone replied. 'Do you think Oliver has ADHD?'

Dr Munchie said no. She said it sounded very much like Oliver was in fact a highly evolved Indigo child – a divine being with enormously heightened spiritual wisdom and psychic powers. Oliver couldn't concentrate, she explained, because he was being distracted by genuine psychic experiences. She said Indigo children were springing up all over the world, all at once, unconnected to one another. There were tens of thousands of them, in every country. And their parents weren't all New Age hippies. There were perfectly ordinary families who were realizing how super-evolved and psychic their children were. This was a global phenomenon. Soon the Indigo children would rise up and heal the planet.

Perhaps, Dr Munchie said, given this new diagnosis, Simone and Oliver might like to attend an Indigo children meeting at the Moat House Hotel in Bedford? Channel 4 was going to be there. Maybe the TV crew could follow Oliver about?

Simone was desperate for answers. She wasn't

going to close off any avenue. So that's how she and Oliver ended up appearing in the Channel 4 documentary *My Kid's Psychic*.

It is a badly named programme. Oliver isn't psychic. He has ADHD. I telephone Simone after watching a tape of the programme. She tells me he's responding well to cod-liver-oil tablets. In the documentary, Simone looks bewildered to be at the Indigo conference, which seems like an incongruous mix of hippies and spiritualists and perfectly ordinary but frazzled families like hers.

'That woman, Dr Munchie, seemed to be running it,' Simone says. 'Some of the people there were really away with the fairies. Most of them were. "I see this and I see that." One man was saying his children were "the best people ever". I don't want my child being called an Indigo child, thank you very much.'

Still, Simone doesn't regret appearing in the programme: 'It really helped Oliver enormously to learn that other people see things.'

I'm curious to know more about the Indigo children – this apparently vast, underground movement. Although Indigos say they communicate telepathically, they also communicate via Internet forums, like Indigos Unplugged, which is where I discover a twenty-one-question quiz: 'Is Your Child An Indigo?'

I decide to take it on Joel's behalf:

Does your child have difficulty with discipline and authority?
Yes.

Does your child refuse to do certain things they [sic] *are told to do?*
Yes, he bloody well does.

Does your child get frustrated with systems that don't require creative thought [such as spelling and times tables]?
Yes. This is getting eerie.

Does your child display symptoms of Attention Deficit Disorder?
No.

Is your child very talented (may be identified as gifted)?
Of course!

Does your child have very old, deep, wise looking eyes?
No.

'If you have more than fifteen yes answers,' it says at the bottom, 'your child is almost definitely Indigo.'

Joel has sixteen yes answers.

'Realize that if you are the parent of one of

these spirits you have been given a wonderful, mar-
vellous gift! Feel honoured that they have chosen
you and help them develop to their fullest Indigo
potential.'

I decide not to tell Joel that I'm honoured he's
chosen me. It might turn him into a nightmare.

I track down Dr Munchie. She lives in Derbyshire. I
call her. She sounds very nice. She says it was the
American author Lee Carroll who first identified the
Indigos in his 1999 book *The Indigo Children: The
New Kids Have Arrived*. The book sold 250,000
copies. Word spread, to Ipswich amongst other places,
where Dr Munchie was working as a GP within the
Government's Sure Start programme.

'Sure Start is designed to give underprivileged children the best start in life,' Dr Munchie explains. 'One
mum came in talking about it. And I immediately saw
how important it was.'

Even though Dr Munchie is a GP – that most
pragmatic of professions – she's always been secretly
spiritual, ever since she had a 'kundalini experience'
whilst doing yoga during her medical-school years. (A
kundalini experience is a spiritual awakening that
sometimes occurs during yoga.) And that's how she
became an Indigo organizer.

But, she says, I happen to be looking at the movement during a somewhat rocky period for them.

'There have been lots of reports of parents saying to teachers, "You can't discipline my child. She's an Indigo,"' Dr Munchie says. 'So it's all a bit controversial at the moment.'

'Do you sometimes think, "What have I helped to unleash?"' I ask her.

She replies that in fact she sees herself as a moderate force in the movement: 'For instance, lots of people think all children who have ADHD are Indigo children. I just think some are.'

My guess is that the weird success of the Indigo movement is a result of a growing public dissatisfaction with the pharmaceutical industry. It's certainly true in the case of Simone, Oliver's mum. Simone told me that all the doctors ever really wanted to do with Oliver was dope him up with Ritalin.

'Ritalin didn't help him,' Simone told me. Then she added, sharply: 'All it did was keep him quiet.'

No wonder that when Dr Munchie approached Simone at that party she was open to any idea, however nutty-sounding.

Novartis, the drug company that manufactures Ritalin, say that in 2002, 208,000 doses of Ritalin were prescribed in the UK. That's up from 158,000 in 1999, which was up from 127,000 in 1998, which was up from a paltry 92,000 in 1997.

I call Martin Westwell, Deputy Director of the Oxford University think tank the Institute for the Future of the Mind. I tell him about these statistics.

'You've got two kids in a class,' he explains. 'One has ADHD. For that kid, Ritalin is absolutely appropriate. It turns their life around. The other kid is showing a bit of hyperactivity. That kid's parents see the drug working on the other kid. So they go to their GP . . .' Martin pauses. 'In some ways there's a benefit to being diagnosed with ADHD,' he says. 'You get a statement of special needs. You get extra help in class . . .'

And this, he says, is how the culture of over-diagnosis, and over-prescription of Ritalin-type drugs, has come to be. Nowadays, one or two children in every classroom across the US are on medication for ADHD, and things are going this way in the UK too.

Indigo believers look at the statistics in another way. They say it is proof of an unprecedented psychic phenomenon.

On Friday night I attend a meeting of Indigo children in the basement of a spiritualist church in the suburbs of Chatham, Kent. The organizer is medium Nikki Harwood, who also features in the documentary *My Kid's Psychic*. (Nikki's daughter Heather is Indigo.) Nikki picks me up at Chatham station.

'There have been reports of Indigo children trying to commit suicide – they're so ultra-sensitive to feelings,' Nikki tells me en route in her people carrier. 'Imagine having the thoughts and feelings of everyone around you in your head. One thing I teach them is how to switch off, so they can have a childhood.' Nikki pauses, and adds: 'In an ideal world, Indigo children would be schooled separately.'

We pull up outside the church. Hoodies slouch around on nearby street corners. Inside, eleven Indigo children sit in a circle.

'One kid here,' Nikki whispers to me, 'his dad is a social worker.'

The youngest here is seven. The oldest is eighteen. His name is Shane. He's about to join the army.

'That doesn't sound very Indigo,' I say.

'Oh, it is,' Nikki replies. 'Indigos need structure.'

And then the evening begins, with fifteen minutes of boring meditation.

'Allow your angel wings to open,' Nikki tells them, et cetera, and I think: 'I came all the way for this? Meditation?'

But then it gets a lot more interesting.

'I was with a baby the other day,' Nikki informs the class. 'I said, "Hello, sweetheart," with my thoughts. The baby looked at me shocked as if to say, "How did you know we communicate with each other using our thoughts?"'

The Indigo kids smile and nod. Indigo organizers like Nikki and Dr Munchie believe we're all born with these powers. The difference is that the Indigo children don't forget how to use them.

Then Nikki produces a number of blindfolds. She puts them over the eyes of half the children, and instructs them to walk from one end of the room to the other.

The idea is for the un-blindfolded kids to telepathically communicate to the blindfolded ones where the tables and chairs and pillars are. Nikki says this is half an exercise in telepathy, and half an exercise in eradicating fear.

'Part of the reason why you're here,' she tells the children – and by 'here' she means put on this planet as part of a super-evolved Indigo species – 'is to teach the grown-ups not to feel fear.'

The children nod. And the exercise in telepathy begins.

And it gives me no pleasure to say this, but blindfolded children immediately start walking into chairs, into pillars, into tables.

'You're not listening, Zoe!' shouts Nikki at one point, just after Zoe has collided with a chair. 'We were [telepathically] saying "Stop!"'

'I can't hear!' says Zoe.

Still, these children are having far more fun learning about their religion than most children do.

I wander down to the front of the hall. Children's drawings are tacked up on a noticeboard – drawings of past lives.

'I had people that waited on me,' one girl has written next to her drawing of a princess. 'I was kind but strict. Very rich, such as royalty.'

'There's one girl here,' Nikki points out a little girl called Emily, 'who had a real fear of being starved to death.'

Lianne – Emily's mother – comes over to join us.

'She used to hide food all over the house,' Lianne says.

'Anyway,' Nikki says, 'we regressed her, and in the past life she'd been locked in a room by her mum and starved to death.'

'Emily is much better now,' Lianne says, 'since she started coming here.'

Lianne says that – like many parents of Indigo

children – she wasn't in the least bit New Age before the family began attending Indigo meetings. She was perfectly ordinary and sceptical. She heard about the Indigo movement through word of mouth. It seemed to answer the questions she had about her daughter's behaviour. And she's very glad she came.

Nikki says Emily happens to be 'the most Indigo person here, apart from my own daughter. Emily will go into the bathroom and see dead people. She sees them walking around the house. It used to terrify her. Will I introduce you to her?'

Emily is thirteen. She seems like a sweet, ordinary teenage girl. She offers to do a tarot reading for me.

'Something is holding you back,' she says. 'Tying you down. You don't look very happy.'

I'm fine, I think.

'You're a little goldfish,' says Emily. 'Your dream is to turn into a big rainbow fish. It'll be a bumpy ride, but you'll get there. Just don't be scared. You're Paula Radcliffe. You just don't think you are.'

Earlier this year, the *Dallas Observer* ran an article about Indigo children.

One eight-year-old was asked if he was Indigo. The boy nodded, and replied: 'I'm an avatar. I can recognize the four elements of earth, wind, water and fire.'

The journalist was impressed.

After the article ran, several readers wrote in to inform the newspaper of the Nickelodeon show *Avatar: The Last Airbender*. In the cartoon, Avatar has the power to bend earth, wind, water and fire. The *Dallas Observer* later admitted it felt embarrassed about the mistake.

When the Indigo meeting is over, Nikki gives me a lift back to the station.

'Does it freak the children out to be told they're super-evolved chosen ones?' I ask her.

'They were feeling it anyway,' Nikki replies.

We drive on in silence for a moment.

'I've been police-checked,' Nikki says, suddenly. 'Another medium called the police on me. I've been accused of emotionally damaging the children.'

'And what did the police do when they came?' I ask.

'They laughed,' Nikki says. Then she pauses, and adds: 'They told me they wanted to bring their own children here.'

Maybe – I think – they were just saying that to be polite. Or maybe they really meant it.

4. SANTA'S LITTLE CONSPIRATORS

It is a Monday in late October and I'm standing inside a smoke-filled lotto shop in the tiny Alaskan town of North Pole, population 1,600. This shop sells only two things: cigarettes and Lotto scratch cards. Chain-smoking inveterate gamblers sit at the counter and frantically demolish mountains of the scratch cards. They have names like Royal Jackpot, Blame It On Rio and Gentlemen Prefer Blondes. It's a pretty desperate place.

Outside, people are going about their business on Frosty Avenue. Friends are chatting on Kris Kringle Drive. A gang of hoodies are slouched against the candy-cane-striped streetlights on Santa Claus Lane, having just emerged from the Christmas-themed McDonald's.

Everything in North Pole is Christmas-themed. It is Christmas Day here three hundred and sixty-five days a year. The decorations are always up. It never stops being Christmas here. Never. Wherever you are in the world, if you write a letter to Santa, and address it simply 'Santa, North Pole', your letter will most likely end up in this tiny Alaskan town.

Actually, specifically, your Santa letter will end up right here, in this smoke-filled scratch-card and cigarette shop. It's late October, and boxes of them are already piled up on the counter near the fruit machine. They're automatically forwarded here from the post office. I pick an envelope up at random. It has only one word scrawled on it, in a child's handwriting: 'Santa'. It's postmarked Doncaster.

I get talking to Debbie who works here, selling scratch cards to the gamblers. Debbie is herself a chain-smoker, a blousy strawberry-blonde, with a tough, good-looking face. She says she can frequently be found alone in here in floods of tears having just opened yet another heartbreaker.

'Just before you got here,' she says, 'I opened one that said, "Dear Santa. All I want for Christmas is for my mother and father to stop shouting at each other." I just fell apart.'

'We get a lot of "Could you bring my father back from Iraq?"' says Gaby, the shop's owner.

Debbie answers as many Santa letters as she can,

whenever she gets a break. She writes back using her elf name: Twinkle.

And she has help. Each week in November and December, a box of Santa letters is sent over to the nearby middle school, where the town's eleven- and twelve-year-olds – the sixth-graders – write back in the guise of elves. It is part of the curriculum.

But there's something else – something bad. Six of last year's middle-school elves, now aged thirteen, were arrested back in April for being in the final stages of plotting a mass murder, a Columbine-style school shooting. The information is sketchy, but apparently they had elaborate diagrams and code names and lists of the kids they were going to kill. I've come to North Pole to investigate the plot. What turned those elves bad? Were they serious? Was the town just too Christmassy?

I need to tread carefully. So far I've only tried to ask one person about it – James, the waiter in Pizza Hut – and it went down badly.

'North Pole is the greatest place I've ever been,' James told me as he poured my coffee. 'The people here are always ready to do! We stay on track and we move on forward! We don't let anything get us down.

That's the spirit of North Pole and the spirit of Christmas. People here are willing to put their best foot forward and be the best kind of people they can be.'

'I heard about the thing with the kids over at the middle school plotting a Columbine-style massacre,' I said.

At this, James let out a noise the likes of which I've never really heard before. It was a heart-wrenching 'Aaaaaah.' He sounded like a balloon being burst by me, with all the joy escaping from him like air.

'That was a, uh, shock . . .' said James.

'You have to wonder why . . .' I said.

'This is a very happy, cheerful, cheery place,' said James. 'Anything more you need?'

'No,' I said.

And James walked back to the counter, shooting me a sad look, as if to say, 'What kind of a grinch are you to bring that up?'

Monday night. People keep telling me that everybody in North Pole loves Christmas. But I've found someone who doesn't. In fact she hates Christmas. Her name is Jessie Desmond. I found her via MySpace.

'Christmas is a super big deal around here,' she

emailed me before I set off for Alaska, 'but for me it is a general hate. Please don't go off me about that.'

We meet in a non-Christmassy bar of her choice on the edge of town. She's in her early twenties. She was educated at the middle school, and is now trying to make her way as a comic-book artist. She has a Batman logo tattooed on her hand.

'Christmas really grates on me, all the time, in the back of my head,' she tells me. 'Christmas, Christmas, Christmas. It drives me nuts.'

'But there must be something you do like about North Pole,' I say.

Jessie thinks about this. 'Well, if you get into an accident or something, everyone's willing to help you,' she eventually shrugs.

I decide it's safe to ask Jessie – being anti-Christmas – about the mass-murder plot.

'Do you know the boys?' I ask her.

She shakes her head.

'Apparently they drew up a list,' I say.

'Well, I have a hate list on my wall too,' Jessie replies.

'Yes,' I say, 'but I'm sure you don't have access to weapons.'

'I have a revolver in my bedroom,' Jessie says.

'Do you stand in front of the mirror with it and shout "Freeze!" and imagine what it's like to kill your enemies?' I ask.

There's a silence.

'I might,' says Jessie, finally.

I ask Jessie if she'll take me to her house and show me her gun. She agrees. Of course Jessie has no intention of killing anyone, and on the way she tells me she suspects the boys were just like her – all talk – and the town only took them seriously because everyone is terrified of everything these days.

Although this is late October, Jessie's house is extremely Christmassy. Her parents, Mike and Edith (a former Miss Alaska), are enormous Christmas fans.

'Did you see my Christmas balls up front?' Edith asks me. 'The nicest thing about living in North Pole is that you can leave your Christmas decorations up all year.'

'Are there people in North Pole who don't like Christmas?' I ask.

'I don't know any,' says Mike.

I glance at Jessie. She's sitting cross-legged on the floor at their feet, displaying no emotion.

Mike shows me the mounted head of a sheep he once shot. It's wearing tinsel.

'You never think that having decorations up all year round is too much Christmas?' I ask.

Edith shakes her head.

'No,' she says, firmly. 'No. I love Christmas. It's my favourite time.'

'Jessie,' I say. 'Will you show me your gun?'

'Sure,' she says.

I tell Mr and Mrs Desmond that it was lovely to meet them, and I walk with Jessie down the corridor. We pass a row of paintings depicting Santa in various festive settings, in front of log fires, et cetera. Across the corridor is Jessie's bedroom. It is free of anything Christmassy.

'Does your mother know . . . ?' I begin.

'That I don't like Christmas?' says Jessie.

I nod.

'I've told her,' she says. 'But I don't think she believes me.'

She rummages around her wardrobe and pulls out her revolver.

'You're the first person to see it,' she says.

She straightens her arm – a blank look on her face – like in a police movie. She says she sometimes pretends to kill the kids who bullied her in middle school. 'I walk up to them when no one is around and

I bop them over the head and shoot them!' she says. 'Ha ha!'

Jessie says the person I should really ask about the plot is Jeff Jacobson. He teaches sixth grade at the middle school. He must have known the boys. Plus Jeff was Mayor of North Pole until last week. If anyone knows – and is willing to tell – it's Jeff, Jessie says.

And so I leave Jessie's house and I call Jeff Jacobson. He says I'm welcome to visit him tomorrow at the school during the lunch period.

Dusk is settling. One of the town's two giant Santa sculptures – the one outside the RV park – lights up. Eerily, however, it is lit from below, which gives Santa's eyes a hollow, creepy look, like Jack Nicholson in *The Shining*. I get an early night.

Tuesday morning. Apparently the kids who were plotting the shootings were goths. Earl Dolman, the owner of the permanently Christmas decorated Dolman's Diner, the most popular restaurant in town, tells me this. Just about everyone who lives in North Pole eats breakfast at Dolman's. It has a lovely, festive, community feel, even if the decorations are starting to look somewhat frayed and faded.

There's Twinkle the elf – Debbie – who looks like she's been up all night opening letters to Santa and sobbing.

Being a letter-opening elf can really do someone's head in, I think.

There's Mary Christmas, who runs the Santa Claus House gift shop. That's her real name. It's on her birth certificate.

And there's Earl Dolman, the owner of the diner. We get talking.

'Do you know anything about that shooting plot over at the middle school?' I ask him.

'I know the kids were goths,' he says.

'Really?' I say.

Earl gives me a look to say, 'Well, of course they were goths. What else would they be?'

'Where I come from,' I explain, 'goths aren't dangerous.'

'Really?' says Earl, surprised.

'Goths don't do anything bad in the UK,' I say 'They're a gentle and essentially middle-class sub-culture.'

'Huh!' says Earl.

'I suppose the difference is that the goths in Britain aren't armed,' I muse. 'They're so death-obsessed, it's probably good to keep them away from guns.'

Earl gives me a look to say, 'There's nothing wrong with gun ownership.'

Then he tells me that – as a result of the shooting plot – his daughter has pulled her kids out of the middle school. The Dolman kids are being home-schooled instead now.

'It shook everyone up,' says Earl.

I have a few hours to kill before I get to go inside the middle school and meet Jeff Jacobson, and so I visit a sweet, twinkly-eyed lady called Jan Thacker, local columnist and author of the book *365 Days of Christmas: The Story of North Pole*.

Her book begins, 'So does he? Does Santa really live in North Pole? . . . The police chief believes it, and who is more honest than the chief of police?'

Jan and I chat for a while, and then she takes me into her back room, which is full of guns – a glinting rack of them – and a number of stuffed wolves she's killed.

The stuffed wolves have ferocious facial expressions. They're snarling, their teeth bared, their eyes aflame with hatred, ready to pounce.

I tell Jan she must have been very brave to shoot those terrifying wolves.

'Were they really pouncing like that when you shot them?' I ask.

There's a short silence.

'No,' Jan says.

Then she explains: the local taxidermist, Charlie Livingstone, tends to give the wolves ferocious expressions however they were behaving at the moment of their death – even if they were just wandering around all doe-eyed, looking for a pat and a play.

It's surprising to see such a twinkly-eyed old lady so heavily armed, but this is normal for North Pole. It solves the mystery of where the plotters would have got the guns. There are guns everywhere.

This is mainly because of all the bears. There are bears everywhere, and moose. I suspect this is why the town is so Republican. There are virtually no liberals. When you've got that many bears, you're not going to be liberal. You know what liberals are like with bears. We just scream. We let out a high-pitched scream and run away, our arms in the air.

It is all the more surprising, then, that Jeff Jacobson is a gentle-hearted liberal, a card-carrying Democrat. I've been told that sometimes, at night, Jeff can be seen driving around North Pole quietly putting up decorations in underprivileged parts of town. Now it is lunchtime, and Jeff is putting up decorations in his maths classroom. He's wearing a Santa hat and a tie covered in snowmen. We talk a little about how much he misses being mayor.

I don't think Jeff gets on with the new mayor, Doug Isaacson, who's apparently a steely-eyed, shaven-headed staunch Bush Republican. Doug Isaacson's big idea is apparently to get all the shopkeepers in town to wear elf costumes as a means of generating increased tourist revenue. Jeff feels this is just window-dressing, and what's on the inside is what counts, Christmas-wise.

Jeff tells me this is a good week for me to be in North Pole. Tomorrow his sixth-graders will get their first ever batch of Santa letters to answer. They'll give themselves elf names and write back on Santa's behalf.

'We live in a world of text messaging and video games,' Jeff says. 'Being a Santa's elf connects us with real people all around the world.'

'Can I come along and watch them do it?' I ask.

'Of course,' Jeff says.

'Jeff,' I say. 'I hear some of last year's elves were caught plotting a mass-murder.'

For a second Jeff freezes, Christmas decorations in hand. Then he recovers, and carries on pinning them up.

'It was going to be on a Monday,' he says.

'How was it thwarted?' I ask.

'One of the kids – the one who was going to be bringing the weapons in – didn't show up that day,' Jeff says, 'and so they postponed the plan. And while they were discussing the postponement, the plan was overheard, and the police intervened.'

'And what was the plan?' I ask.

'They were going to bring some knives and guns in,' he says, 'and they were going to kill students and teachers. They were going to disrupt the telephone system. They knew where the telephone controls were. And they were also going to disable the electricity. Turn off the lights. And carry out their plans. And these were well-thought-out plans. They had diagrams. They had a list . . .'

'How many people were on the list?' I ask.

'Dozens,' says Jeff. 'And each kid was assigned who was going to do who. With what.'

'Oh my God,' I say.

Jeff shrugs. Then he smiles.

'Saying all that,' he says, 'these boys had just turned thirteen years old. They were going to disable the telephone system. That sounds terrifying, right? Well . . .'

Jeff rummages around in his pocket and pulls out

his mobile phone. He gives me a look to say, 'Well, duh!'

'So maybe they once saw someone in a James Bond movie disable a building's communications system,' he says.

The more Jeff tells me about the ins and outs of the plot, the more it strikes me as a mix of very chilling and very stupid. For instance, after the shootings, Jeff says, the boys were going to run to the station and catch a train to Anchorage, where they'd create new lives for themselves using aliases. One boy's alias was going to be John Wayne.

The thing is, they hadn't checked the train time-tables. The shootings were going to occur at lunchtime in the cafeteria. Even if they gave themselves an hour to kill their enemies and get to the station, they would still have had a five-hour wait on the platform for the Anchorage train.

It was an ill-thought-out plan.

Lunchtime is over, and Jeff's sixth-graders run into class. Some gasp, thrilled, at the Christmas decorations. They are only twelve, just a few months younger than the plotters, and they look like little children.

'To see those little boys in handcuffs,' Jeff says. 'I taught five of them. It broke my heart. As teachers we had to carry on like it was a normal day. But we were being ravaged inside with our emotions. Some teachers were having anxiety attacks. One is still suffering badly with stress . . .'

I wonder if the whole thing was just kids' talk and they were never really planning to commit mass-murder. Maybe it was just a fantasy to them, no more real than the Christmas fantasy is to the adults here, or the fantasy of the ferocious wolves is to Jan, the twinkly-eyed huntswoman. I'm not allowed by law to meet the kids, but I'm determined to meet at least one of their parents this week. I ask Jeff if he'll try and arrange this. He promises he will. I tell him I'll see him tomorrow afternoon for letter-opening elf class.

Wednesday morning. Doug Isaacson – the new Mayor of North Pole – stands atop a snowy nature trail and surveys his town below.

'Imagine being in England two thousand years ago when your towns were just getting started,' Doug says. 'How would you set them up for future generations?'

Doug pauses. There's a look of real passion in his eyes.

'That's where we are!' he says. 'We can do that here! That's awesome.'

'How old is North Pole?' I ask.

'Fifty years old,' says Doug.

'You're a founding father,' I say.

'Very much so,' says Doug. 'And we'll be forgotten to history in time. But not the things we start. Not the things we set up properly. They'll last a lot longer.'

This is Doug's first week in office. He says he was elected on a Christmas mandate. His campaign centred on the proposition that whilst North Pole is very Christmassy, there is room for it to be even more Christmassy. Recently, Doug went on a fact-finding visit to the small Washington town of Leavenworth, where everything is Bavarian-themed. Many shop-keepers there wear lederhosen and sell bratwurst.

As a result, Doug has had an idea. It is an idea he recognizes will be a hard sell to the people of this freedom-loving wilderness town. But the idea is this: Doug would like the shopkeepers of North Pole to wear elf costumes. He wants North Pole to be a fully-fledged theme town, with a Santa's Secret Village and lots of townspeople wandering around dressed as elves.

'Many people move to Alaska because they don't want to be fenced in,' I say. 'So if you say, "I'm going to fence you in with elf costumes . . ." Might that be an issue?'

'Absolutely,' says Doug. 'But let me show you something.'

We climb into Doug's pickup truck. He drives me around town.

'Some people,' Doug says, 'think North Pole looks like a truck stop. And that's unconscionable.'

We drive past the extremely festive Dolmans Diner, but then past the utterly non-Christmassy computer shop cum video-game arcade, where I see teenagers playing incredibly violent shooting games.

Doug says he has half a mind to turn up un-announced at the not-Christmassy-enough businesses, introduce himself as the new mayor and ask the owners to start wearing elf costumes.

'We should *do* it!' I say, enthusiastically.

And so we do.

We enter the computer shop cum video arcade – in the mall next to Safeway – where half a dozen teenage boys are shooting the hell out of the SAS. It is a computerized bloodbath. British soldiers' heads are exploding. Blood sprays from their backs as they lie convulsing in the desert dirt.

Doug walks purposefully past the boys and towards the owner. He produces an elf costume from his bag. Doug doesn't have to say anything. The owner instinctively knows where this is heading.

'No,' he says.

'Will you at least try the hat on?' Doug asks.

'No,' he says.

Doug tries to appeal to him entrepreneur to entre-preneur. Apparently North Pole has recently lost a big Alaska Airlines promotion. For the past two years, the airline flew tourists into North Pole and took them dog-sledging, Christmas-ornament making and so on. But this year, Alaska Airlines has decided that North Pole just doesn't look Christmassy enough.

'If we want to capture that Christmassy tourist,' Doug says unapologetically, 'then, yeah, for at least six weeks out of the year people ought to wear elf suits.'

The computer-shop owner says he'll think about it.

I drift away and get talking to one of the teenage boys. He's spraying an SAS officer up the back with a machine gun.

'Do you ever get an overdose of Christmas, living here?' I ask him.

'Pretty much all summer,' he says.

'What do you do to redress the balance?' I ask.

'I come here and shoot people all day,' he shrugs.

'Doug,' I say, as we leave the computer shop, 'do you think that if the town had been more Christmassy back in April, those kids at the middle school wouldn't have wanted to plot their Columbine-style massacre?'

'Let's just say that if the spirit of Christmas were permeating the entire soul of this community, no child would be feeling that despondent,' Doug replies. 'What is the spirit of Christmas? Isn't it peace on Earth? Good will to men?'

Doug seems idealistic about imposing elf costumes on the shopkeepers of North Pole. He seems to believe absolutely in the power of the markets to heal all wounds.

Wednesday lunchtime. I call Jessie Desmond, my North Pole MySpace friend who hates Christmas.

'Guess what I'm about to do,' I say. 'I'm going to the middle school to watch the sixth-graders open their first-ever batch of Santa letters. Do you remember your first batch of Santa letters?'

There's a silence.

'It was one of my first moments of real disappointment,' she says.

'Sorry?' I say.

'You learn really fast that Santa doesn't exist,' says Jessie.

'You're kidding,' I say.

But Jessie isn't. She explains: the town keeps the practice a secret from the younger children. They have no idea that they'll one day – at the age of eleven or twelve – be obliged to become letter-writing elves. She says it can be quite a shock.

Jessie says it isn't as bad as it could be. They do have rules: 'If someone writes something like, "Dear Santa, my mom has cancer. Can you make it go away?" we don't deal with those. We give them back to the teacher.'

But still, she says, it's a disappointment.

'Most of the kids say they're OK with it,' she says, 'but you know they're not. Because there we were thinking something was up there, but in sixth grade we realize there's nothing. It's just us up there.'

Jessie pauses. 'I had written letters to Santa with really personal things in them. I told Santa I wanted a baby sister. The idea that some sixth-grade kids had read that. And suddenly you're in sixth grade, and you have this batch of letters on your desk and you're writing back: "Yes, Santa's happy with you. Yes, you're going to get what you asked for." It really ruined it for me. I felt like I was doing Santa's dirty work.'

'Are you telling me that I'm about to go to middle

school to watch a bunch of children be confronted, for the first time in their lives, with the possibility that Santa doesn't exist?' I ask.

'Yes,' Jessie says. 'You'll probably see it in their faces. They prepare you for a few weeks before, but there's always that one person who's like, "Wait. What are we doing?" And that's the person you should be looking out for. The person who wasn't paying attention in class until the letters are right in front of them. And then they're shattered. It's a weird experience.'

And so it is with a nervous feeling that I drive to middle school at lunchtime. In the classroom, Jeff hands out Christmas hats. He asks his children to think up elf names. And then he distributes the Santa letters. Of course I'm doing what Jessie told me to – scrutinizing the faces of the children for some evidence of hope dying – but I don't see anything like it. In fact they all seem quite excited.

Contrary to what Jessie said, Jeff instructs his elves not to write 'Santa is going to give you everything you asked for'. Instead he tells them to be more vague: 'I'm sure you'll like whatever surprises you find under your tree. From all the elves at North Pole, and from

Santa, Merry Christmas, and remember it's always better to be good than bad.'

A dark cloud only settles over the room once, when one little boy reads out a letter that says, 'Dear Santa, this year I would like to wear a lot of clothes and shoes, but my mom can't buy us a lot of clothes because she gets paid a little bit and she pays a lot of rent. Santa, that is my wish for Christmas. I know it may seem a lot for you but that is all I want for Christmas. To wear a lot of clothes.'

Later, after the children go home, I ask Jeff, 'Do you ever get a kid saying, "Hang on. If we're opening the letters, what does that say about . . . ?"'

'Santa?' says Jeff. 'Well, at eleven and twelve they're pretty savvy. They all know that Santa is basically mom and dad.'

I give Jeff a quizzical look.

Jeff gives me a look back that says, 'Don't be silly.'

Still, I can't help wondering if Jeff has inadvertently made a mistake getting his sixth-graders to be letter-opening elves. My week in North Pole has made me suspect that the job can mess you up. There's poor Twinkle in the Lotto shop, constantly in tears, powerless to help. Then there's Jessie, realizing that if she was the magic, then the magic was rubbish. Jessie told me she wouldn't be surprised if the plotters were set in part on their nihilistic path as a result of being letter-opening elves.

That night, back at the hotel, the telephone rings. It's a man's voice. He says his name is Joe.

'My son was one of the ringleaders,' he says.

Joe says he's willing to talk to me, but not at his house. I call Jeff. He says we can use the middle school.

And so that's when I meet Joe, on Saturday morning, in the deserted cafeteria in the deserted middle school.

Joe's a soldier. 'I was in Iraq when I got the word,' he says.

'Whereabouts were you?' I ask.

'South of Basra,' Joe says. 'I'd been there quite a few months.'

Joe says he was in the habit of chatting with his wife online early each morning, and one morning in April she typed into the chat box, 'I've got to tell you something. We need to talk about Jack.'

Jack isn't the boy's real name. He had just turned thirteen in April.

'He's OK,' typed Joe's wife. 'There's nothing physically wrong.'

'I thought maybe he skipped a few days of school or something,' says Joe.

But, instead, Joe's wife typed the news that Jack had got involved with a group of boys, and they had made a list, and Jack was 'highly involved' with this, and their plan was to kill the kids on the list, and to do it in the cafeteria.

As Joe relays this to me, I look up with a start. This is where we're sitting: in the school cafeteria. For an instant I imagine it.

'Were they serious?' I ask.

'I've asked my son that point-blank,' Joe replies. 'I said, "Would you have done this?" He said, "Yes. I would have." And he maintains that to this day. He says they would have done it.'

Joe pauses.

'They were going to fire some warning shots,' he says. 'There were other kids that were indirectly involved – they'd been told about the plan: they were to get certain other kids out of the cafeteria when the warning shots were fired. My son was to go to the office with a rifle and disable the communications equipment, and then they were going to start shooting the kids from the list.'

'How many kids were on the list?' I ask.

'Fifteen or twenty,' Joe says. 'And there was a comment on there: "And all the other cool kids." Who knows what that means? That's kind of open-ended, right? That's kind of subjective.'

After Joe's wife told Joe the news of the plot, via the chat box, Joe sought emergency leave. He says it was hard to leave Iraq.

'I had a sense of responsibility to my comrades,' he says. 'You want to come home with your unit.'

Sometimes, during our interview, Joe sounds like a soldier making a report to his commanding officer. He says things like, 'At this time my son stated to me . . .' and so on. But there are other occasions when he's doing all he can to stop himself from breaking down in tears. I think he thinks he can conceal his broken heart better than he actually can.

Jack was in custody when Joe returned from Iraq. The charge was conspiracy to commit first-degree murder.

'I really didn't know how to react,' he says. 'Part of me wanted to grab him and shake him and say, "What is your problem?" And the other part wanted to hug him and say, "We'll protect you from this."'

'What did you do?' I ask.

'I gave him a hug,' Joe says. 'I said, "I love you," and then I said, "Sit down." I could tell he was kind of scared. I asked him, "Why would you do this?" He said, "I don't know."'

Joe says he doesn't know either. It's not like Jack's a goth, he says.

'Oh, so he's not a goth,' I say.

'He likes to fish,' says Joe. 'He likes to go camping. He likes to make up his own jokes. The counsellor is trying to figure out why they'd do this. These kids don't fit the mould. He doesn't come from a dysfunctional family. I mean, we have our dysfunctions, but he's not abused. I don't use drugs. I don't consider myself an alcoholic. I spend time with him. I coached baseball for him when he was younger.'

Joe pauses. 'We have rules. He doesn't dress goth. He's not allowed to dress goth. He's not allowed to have baggy pants that hang down. He's not allowed to wear his hat cocked to the side and walk around looking like a little punk. We never let him have violent posters on his walls. He's not allowed to play violent video games. He's never been to the mall by himself. He doesn't have any CDs, like rap CDs, with violent themes. That kind of stuff just doesn't fit in with our lives.'

As Joe says this, I think about my eight-year-old

son, Joel. I always let him wear his baseball cap cocked to one side. He has a *Kill Bill* poster on his wall. He listens to Eminem.

My God, I think in a panic. If Jack was going to kill everyone in his school *without* all those violent influences, what the hell is Joel going to grow up to be?

But then I think, Or maybe it was the absence of all those violent influences that led Jack to want to commit mass-murder.

Or could it have been the town's Christmas theme? The elf business?

'I guess that theory is as good as any theory,' Joe shrugs. 'The doctors and the counsellors have no answers. I have no answers. The boy himself has no answers.'

Then there's the other possibility: that Joe's months away fighting in Iraq – helping to impose democracy – did something to his son's psyche.

Joe sighs.

'Maybe,' he says.

North Pole has been hit hard by Iraq. At the end of September, two soldiers in full-dress uniform arrived at the home of one of Joe's neighbours, Donna Thornton, to tell her that her twenty-four-year-old son James had recently died from a cardiac arrest in Baghdad.

James had been at the middle school, a year or two above Jessie.

And there have been others. Joseph Love-Fowler – who was twenty-two and in the same year as Jessie – was blown up by a roadside bomb in Balad in April. North Pole has a smallish military base, Fort Wainwright, on its borders. Fort Wainwright has so far lost twenty-six soldiers in Iraq.

Or maybe being thirteen, and being picked on, was reason enough. Everyone behaves irrationally when they reach thirteen. I suppose it is a statistical inevitability that some bullied thirteen-year-olds, somewhere, will be plotting a school shooting. (I, personally, don't have much sympathy for the bullying motive. There were six ringleaders, and seven others with knowledge of the plot. That makes fifteen. So they can hardly call themselves bullied outcast loners. Fifteen is more friends than I ever had.)

Joe often wonders what might have happened had the guns reached the school. This is the only reason why the plot failed: the boy who was supposed to bring the guns didn't turn up.

Apparently, Jack behaved perfectly normally over breakfast that Monday morning. He was joking around as usual, even though he believed that within a few hours he was to commit mass murder.

Joe looks around the cafeteria.

'His sister goes here,' he says. 'I said to him, "Did you tell her, so she could get out when the shooting started?" And he said, "No." I said, "What if your sister heard the shooting, worried about you, ran to see what you were doing and one of the kids shot her?" And I could see from the look on his face that those thoughts had never crossed his mind. He said to me, "We were just going to shoot the bad kids." And I said, "Bullets don't care who they hit or who they kill. They go through people. They tear flesh and they go through. It doesn't matter who's on the other side." He had not thought about that. It was not in his thought process.'

Then Joe mentions the ill-thought-out escape plan – how the kids were going to start new lives in Anchorage.

'To even think they were going to get out of the school without being killed by the police,' he says.

In the end, Jack got off lightly: two years' probation, a five-thousand-word essay on the effects of school shootings across America, a hundred hours of community service, some anger-management therapy.

Joe says he's pleased and relieved nobody has thrown a brick through their window.

'I don't want people taking the law into their own hands,' he says, 'because I have an obligation to protect my son and the rest of my family. So if they push I'm going to have to push back. And if that happens, it's not going to be pretty.'

But he's sending his son back to school next year: 'I told him, "You have to face this. You have to face the kids on that list."'

Joe takes his son out running each morning. Back in April, Jack could barely run half a mile. Now he's running a mile and a half.

Joe looks proud when he tells me this.

There's a school for excluded children on the edge of North Pole. The kids who – for whatever reason – don't fit into the middle school end up studying here. It's quite possible that some of the plotters will join the school next April, when their year's expulsion from the public-school system is up. It seems a great place: small, bright open-plan classrooms and lovely teachers, like Suze, who shows me around. Suze is another rare liberal in a town full of staunch Republicans. I notice that this is one of the very few buildings in town that hasn't any Christmas decorations whatsoever.

'We're a respite from Christmas, I guess,' Suze explains. 'Our kids are all Christmassed out.'

Then I ask Suze a question I've been asking everyone this week.

'Do you happen to know,' I ask, 'where Kris Kringle is?'

Before I arrived in town, I kept hearing stories of an
amazing North Pole resident who looks just like Santa
and has changed his name by deed poll to Kris Kringle.
I heard he was in permanent residence at the local
Santa Claus House gift shop. But when I visited the
place on Monday, I saw that his chair was empty.
Since then, I've been asking everyone: where is Kris
Kringle?

Jeff Jacobson said he thought Kris Kringle had had
some recent falling out with Santa Claus House – 'I
think he was demanding more hot chocolate and
cookies,' he said – and he is now a kind of roving
Santa around town, surprising children in diners and
so on with cries of, 'Ho! Ho! Ho!'

Gaby, who runs the Lotto scratch-card and cigarette shop, said, 'He comes in occasionally, so he
might surprise us. He could pop in at any time.'

'Does he gamble?' I asked.

'Yes,' said Gaby.

James at the Pizza Hut said, 'He was up working
at the Hot Springs last time I heard.'

But the people at the Hot Springs said they hadn't seen him.

Charlie Livingstone, the taxidermist, told me he got hit by a car but he's fine now.

My hunt for Kris Kringle was proving fruitless. People kept telling me they'd just seen him, and he was a wonderful man, but I never saw him. I began to wonder if he even existed. And then I visited the school for excluded children on the edge of town.

'Do you know where Kris Kringle is?' I ask Suze, the teacher.

She looks a little awkward and shuffles uneasily on her feet.

'Have you looked him up on the Internet?' she says.

'No?' I say.

'I think he – uh – died,' says Suze.

'No,' I say. 'That's impossible. People keep telling me they just saw him.'

'I'm sorry to break it to you,' Suze says, 'and it might be the absence of Christmas decorations that allows me to say this, but I think Santa is dead. He passed away this summer.'

There is a silence.

'Well, the taxidermist did say he was hit by a car,'

I say. 'But he also said he recovered fine.' I pause. 'Does everyone know and they're not saying?'

'They might know and they don't want to say,' nods Suze.

'Like a town-wide conspiracy?' I say.

'Maybe,' says Suze. She looks a little embarrassed.

'I am amazed,' I say. 'All this week people I've become good friends with have been looking me in the eye and saying, "I'm sure I saw him a couple of days ago."'

'I can't believe I'm the only person to have owned up to it,' says Suze. She sighs. 'The one that burst the bubble. I hope they don't ride me out of town.'

In the end I go to the library and find conflicting reports from the local paper. One report says Kris Kringle survived a car crash this summer and moved south. The other report says he died in the car crash. I never do find out for certain whether Kris Kringle is alive or not.

It is Sunday, my last day in North Pole. Today, finally, a new Santa will be occupying the vacant seat at Santa Claus House. It seems churlish for me not to go over to say hello.

And when I do, I practically gasp. He is a fantastic

Santa. He looks exactly as Santa should. The setting is perfect: a red velvet chair, presents piled up under the tree, et cetera. Santa's helper Cerys the elf is here too, in a pink elf suit, with pink circles painted on her cheeks.

I introduce myself to Cerys. My plane home is in a few hours, and so Cerys is my last chance of finding out whether Kris Kringle is alive or dead. She'd know, because she would have been his elf when he used to work here.

'Cerys,' I say. 'Do you know where Kris Kringle is?'

'I do,' she says, a big smile on her face.

'Oh!' I say.

'He's right here in Santa Claus House,' says Cerys.

'Oh?' I say, looking around. 'Where?'

'He's right on that chair over there,' says Cerys.

She points at the new Santa.

'That's Kris Kringle,' says Cerys. 'That's Santa. They're one and the same. OK?'

'I understand,' I say. 'Sorry.'

Cerys shoots me a slightly steely look. I recognize the look. It says, 'Don't ask any more questions. Kris Kringle may or may not be dead, but Santa never dies, and that's what matters.'

Then she introduces me to Santa.

'Do you remember Jon when he was a little boy?' she asks him.

'Oh yes,' Santa says. 'I remember Jon. He took a little convincing that I was real.'

'That's *true*!' I say. 'Very early on, when I was four, I told the rest of my class that you didn't exist.'

Santa gasps. 'Come here,' he says. 'Pull my beard.'

I do. 'It's real,' I say.

'And what town are you in?' Santa asks.

'North Pole,' I say.

'And this particular building is . . . ?'

'Santa Claus House,' I say.

'So,' says Santa. 'If you're in a *real* North Pole, in a *real* Santa Claus House and Santa has a *real* beard, that must make me . . .'

'Real!' I say.

Most of the children here are very young, but there are two older girls in the crowd. I ask them how old they are.

'Thirteen,' they say.

That's the same age as the plotters. I remember what Jessie said about how being a letter-writing elf at the age of twelve ruined her belief in Santa, and then I remember what Jeff Jacobson said about how kids of that age are savvy, and they know fact from fantasy.

So I decide to put it to the test.
'Do you believe in Santa?' I ask them.
There is a long silence.
'Half and half,' says one.
'Yes,' says the other.

PART TWO

HOW STUPID DO THEY
THINK WE ARE?

5. WHO KILLED RICHARD CULLEN?

It is a wet February day in a very smoky room in a terraced cottage in Trowbridge, Wiltshire. A portable TV in an alcove plays the news. Everything in here is quite old. No spending spree has taken place in this house. There are wedding and baby and school photographs scattered around. Six children, now all grown up, were raised here. There's a framed child's painting in the toilet, a picture of Wendy Cullen. It reads 'Supergran'. When I phoned Wendy a week ago she said I was welcome to visit, 'Just as long as you don't mind cigarette smoke. I'm smoking myself to death here.'

The '*Congratulations! You have been pre-approved for a loan*' type junk mail is still pouring through their letterbox. Wendy has just thrown another batch in the bin.

'You know what the post is like,' she says.

'I don't get all that much credit-card junk mail,'

I say. 'I get some, I suppose, but not nearly as much as you do.'

'Really?' says Wendy. 'I assumed everyone was constantly bombarded.'

'Not me,' I say.

We both shrug to say, that's a mystery.

It was a month ago today that Wendy's husband, Richard, committed suicide. It was the end of what had been an ordinary twenty-five-year marriage. They met when Wendy owned a B&B on the other side of Trowbridge. He turned up one day and rented a room. Richard had trained to be an electrical engineer but he ended up as a mechanic.

'He loved repairing people's cars,' Wendy says. Then she narrows her eyes at my line of questioning and makes me promise that I am not here to write 'a slushy horrible mawky love story'.

'I'm really not,' I say.

So Wendy continues. Everything was normal until six years ago, when she needed an operation.

'I couldn't face the Royal United,' she says, 'so I went private. I took out a £4,000 loan.'

She says she remembers a time when it was hard for people like them to get loans, but this was easy. Companies were practically throwing money at them.

'Richard handled all the finances. He said, "I can get you one with 0% interest and after six months we'll switch you to another one."'

But then, a few months after the first operation, Wendy was diagnosed with breast cancer and Richard had to take six weeks off to drive her to radiotherapy. The bills needed paying and so, once again, he did that peculiarly modern British thing. He began signing up for credit cards, behaving like a company, thinking he could beat the lenders at their own game by cleverly rolling the debts over from account to account.

We, more than any other country, see this as the answer. There are currently eight million more credit cards in circulation in Britain than there are people: sixty-seven million credit cards, fifty-nine million people.

He signed up with Mint: 'Apply for your Mint Card. You'd need a seriously good reason not to. What's stopping you?'

And Frizzell: 'A name you can trust.'

And Barclaycard: 'Wake up to a fresh start.'

And Morgan Stanley: 'Choose from our Flags of Great Britain range of card designs.'

And American Express: 'Go on, treat yourself.'

And so on.

Right now nobody knows how Richard Cullen's shrewd acumen fell apart.

'He wasn't a man that talked a great deal,' says Wendy, 'and he never, ever discussed finances with me.' But somehow it all spiralled out of control.

Wendy first got the inkling that something was wrong just before Christmas 2004, when the debt-collection departments of various credit-card companies began phoning. He called them back out of his wife's hearing.

'You know how men will walk around with their mobiles,' says Wendy. 'He used to go out into the garden.'

She looks over to the garden behind the conservatory extension and says, 'He was a very proud man. He must have been going through hell. They were very, very persistent. I don't think he was even phoning them back in the end.'

Finally, he admitted it to his wife. He said he didn't seek out all of the twenty-two credit cards he had somehow ended up acquiring between 1998 and 2004. On many occasions they just arrived through the letterbox in the form of '*Congratulations! You have been pre-approved* . . . ' junk. He said he thought he owed about £30,000. There had been no spending spree, he said, no secret vices. He had just tied himself up in knots, using each card to pay off the interest and the charges on the others. The fog of late-payment fees and so on had somehow crept up and engulfed him. He got a pair of scissors from the kitchen and cut up ten credit cards in front of her.

On 10 January 2005 Richard visited his ex-wife, Jennifer, who later told the police that he seemed 'very quiet, like he'd retreated into himself, like his mind was gone.'

She asked him how his weekend was. He replied, 'Not very good.'

Then he went missing for two days.

'Nobody knows where he went,' says Wendy.

On the morning of 12 January, Wendy's son Christopher looked in the garage. It was padlocked so he broke in with a screwdriver. There was an old Vauxhall Nova covered with a sheet.

'I don't know why,' Christopher later told the police, 'but I decided to look under the sheet.'

Richard Cullen had gassed himself in his car. He left his wife a note: 'I just can't take this any more and you'll be better off without me.'

What I want to know is, who killed Richard Cullen?

For instance: why did so many credit-card companies choose to swamp the Cullens with junk when they don't swamp me? How did they even get their address? How can I even begin to find something complicated like that out?

And then I have a brainwave. I'll devise an experiment, I think. I'll create a number of personas. Their surnames will all be Ronson, and they'll all live at my address, but they'll have different first names. Each Ronson will be poles apart, personality-wise. Each will have a unique set of hopes, desires, predilections, vices and spending habits, reflected in the various mailing lists they'll sign up to – from Porsche down to hardcore pornography. The one thing that'll unite them is that they won't be at all interested in credit cards. They will not seek loans nor any financial services as they wander around, filling out lifestyle surveys and entering competitions and purchasing things by mail order. Whenever they're invited to tick a box forbidding whichever company from passing their details to other companies, they'll neglect to tick the box.

Which, if any, of my personas will end up getting sent credit-card junk mail? Which personality type will be most attractive to the credit-card companies?

I name my personas John, Paul, George, Ringo, Dave Dee, Dozy, Beaky, Mick, Titch, Willy, Biff, Happy and Bernard. And I begin.

Happy Ronson

Happy is delightfully ethical. He cares about everything all the time. He has a surfeit of caring. He subscribes to the magazines *Going Green*, *Natural Parenting* and *Vegetarians International Voice For Animals*. He shops at Ecozone and donates to PETA – People for the Ethical Treatment of Animals.

'Happy! What a lovely name!' says the man in the Body Shop on Oxford Street as Happy fills out a Loyalty Card application form.

'Thank you!' I say.

Happy is happy for the Body Shop to pass his details to whoever they see fit. He doesn't tick the box. That's the kind of trusting, positive man he is.

Happy fills in many lifestyle surveys, like the one published by the International Fund for Animal Welfare that asks which animals he especially cares about. Happy especially cares about dogs, cats, elephants, gorillas, tigers, whales, seals, dolphins and all other animals in distress from oil spills. So he ticks everything.

Then I get worried that if anyone is really paying attention to Happy's predilections they might become wary of his wholesale compassion and suspect him of being an imaginary character, created by a journalist, to trick businesses into inadvertently revealing their data-trafficking practices. So I untick tigers.

Paul Ronson

I imagine Paul looks like the kind of guy you see in credit-card adverts, the kind of guy you used to see in cigarette adverts – staggeringly handsome and healthy, fooling around in swimming pools on sunny days with equally beautiful friends.

Paul is an entrepreneur, a suave millionaire, the director of Paul Ronson Enterprises. Being a narcissistic aesthete who can't bear being around ordinary people, he subscribes to *Porsche Design* ('Porsche: The Engineers of Purism'), Priority Pass ('the ultimate privilege for frequent travellers: Escape the crowds to a VIP oasis of calm. Your key to over 450 airport VIP lounges worldwide') and so on.

George Ronson

George Ronson is a charming older gentleman. George orders from the *Daily Express* the CD set *Sentimental Journey*: 'Take a sentimental journey with these 60 everlasting love songs on 4 fabulous CDs . . . Henry Mancini (Moon River) * Glenn Miller (Moonlight Serenade) * Perry Como (Don't Let The Stars Get In Your Eyes) . . .'

'If you do not wish to receive offers from other companies carefully selected by us, please tick this box,' reads the tiniest of letters at the bottom of the order form.

I imagine that George's eyes still have quite the twinkle, but his eyesight isn't what it once was. He is absent-minded and cannot find his glasses, and so he doesn't notice this infinitesimal print.

For this reason, he doesn't tick the box.

George has also entered the Specsavers Spectacle Wearer of the Year competition ('Have You Got Specs Appeal? Our first-prize winner will be awarded a fantastic two-week all-inclusive holiday for two in the Maldives. Send a recent colour photograph of yourself wearing specs to . . .').

I am, unlike George, an embittered cynic, ground down by the travails of life, and so I consequently wonder if this whole spectacle-wearing beauty pageant is an excuse for the company to gather our names and addresses for their database, and to sell them on to other databases.

Titch Ronson

Titch is the least favourite of my personas. He is venal. He is a gullible sex maniac. He thinks about nothing but pornography, his virility, Nazi memorabilia and extreme martial arts. Today Titch takes up an offer in the *News of the World*: 'The original BLUE PILL. Something for the weekend, sir?'

In this newspaper advert, a topless woman wearing a policeman's helmet has a speech bubble that reads, 'Allo, Allo, Allo. What have we here – is it a lethal weapon I see before me?' A warning covers her breasts: 'IMPORTANT NOTICE. Some customers find the 100mg Blue Pill we supply TOO EFFECTIVE. If this happens to you simply reduce usage to half a tablet.'

I assume the Blue Pill is some kind of herbal Viagra. Titch is taken in hook, line and sinker, because he does in fact see his penis as a lethal weapon.

He barely notices a tiny sentence at the bottom of the order form: 'If you don't wish to receive further mailings of exciting offers from us, or associated companies, please tick this box.'

Titch spends his every waking hour seeking depraved gratification and is therefore tantalized by the promise of exciting offers, so he doesn't tick the box. Then he reads the rest of the *News of the World* and is saddened to discover that Kate Moss has got back together with Peter Doherty.

Titch also subscribes to *Fighters Only*, a magazine dedicated to photographs of frequently blood-splattered boxers, with captions like 'Psycho Steve Tetley. Lightweight. Hyper aggressive. He's called Psycho for a reason!'

There is no end to Titch's troubles. He's also, I decide, a hopeless gambling addict, and has signed up to William Hill and the Loopy Lotto free Internet daily draw.

Midway through my experiment I fill in a consumer lifestyle survey on Titch's behalf, attached to a 'Win A Day On A *Playboy* Shoot' competition. ('Get to hang out with girls like this in the flesh! There'll be naked girls! It's a once in an adulthood experience!')

The consumer-lifestyle survey is quite detailed, and so it gives me the opportunity to really flesh out Titch's character and circumstances:

Is Titch in employment?

No. He is an unemployed, single, thirty-eight-year-old homeowner.

His annual earnings are what?

I tick the 'less than £10,000' box.

What are his annual outgoings?

I think for a moment, then tick the '£10,000 – £24,000' box.

So every year Titch somehow manages to spend approximately £14,000 more than he earns.

How frequently does Titch pay off his credit-card balance in full?

Funny question, I think. Titch answers: Rarely.

Then Titch tires of these relentless questions and instead scuttles disgustingly away to order the PABO Sizzling Adult Mail Order Catalogue from their online sex shop. Titch, who thought he had seen it all, is startled by the voluminous choice on offer by PABO. Many of the items for sale involve pumps and studs and – mysteriously – 'tracts' that even the grotesque Titch can't picture aiding a sexual situation.

I put all the things Titch subscribes to in an old picnic hamper, which I keep on a shelf in my office. Rifling through the contents of this picnic hamper is a disturbing experience. Red blood, pink flesh, green baize. Although I have to say that when I troop around the betting offices looking for loyalty schemes for Titch to add his name to, I always stop to play video roulette. It is terribly moreish.

Every morning for three weeks I walk the streets of London in the guise of one or other of my personas. I inevitably spend slightly less time being Titch because I find the prospect of being spotted slouching into sex shops incredibly embarrassing. But by the time the three weeks are up I believe I've been fair and signed each Ronson up to a similar number of lists. And then I wait.

It takes three months for the first unsolicited-loan offer to arrive. And then, suddenly, I am bombarded. And which Ronson is inundated more than any other? Which Ronson receives the first and, in fact, all the credit-card junk mail?

It's Paul: the handsome, high-achieving, aesthetic, sagacious, millionaire Paul.

No, I'm joking. Paul doesn't receive any credit-card junk mail at all.

It's Titch: stupid, superstitious, venal Titch.

Titch has so far been offered loans by Ocean Finance, Shakespeare Finance, Blair Endersby, e-loan-shop.com, TML Mortgage Solutions, loans.co.uk and easyloans.co.uk, and an MBNA Platinum card, and an American Express Red card.

What – I wonder – is Titch's most attractive personality trait for the lenders? Is it his sex addiction, his gambling addiction, his – surely not – interest in bare-knuckle boxing and Nazism? It has to be something. And then I find the culprits! They are in Shoreditch, East London. And they are called Loopy Lotto.

In a splurge of gambling addiction back in April, Titch signed up for the Loopy Lotto free daily Internet draw (top prize £1 million). I remember the occasion well because I had to pick six numbers for him, and so I became – on Titch's behalf – a superstitious fool, choosing numbers that intuitively felt special to me.

You're an irrational gambling-addicted accident waiting to happen, Titch, I thought ruefully to myself as I signed him up.

Last night, as I examined the emails offering Titch 'up to £75,000 for almost any purpose' (loans.co.uk) and 'We will consider all applications, no matter what your credit rating' (Ocean Finance), I noticed that they came via Loopy Lotto.

And so I telephone them.

Dan Bannister – the company's director – sounds lovely, and very surprised to hear from me. He says journalists usually have no interest in what people like him do, because it's terribly boring. But I'm welcome to come over if I like.

The whitewashed loft-style offices of Loopy Lotto could belong to an advertising agency or a TV production company. Boho-yuppies with wire-framed glasses beaver glamorously away as Dan and I sit in the lounge area.

'Who is the average Loopy Lotto subscriber?' I ask him.

'People who are looking for something for nothing and are into instant gratification,' Dan replies. 'It's not a massively upmarket list.'

Dan says they have 600,000 registered players. I say one of them is Titch Ronson.

I tell Dan about my experiment. I explain that my fancy, upmarket personas received no junk mail at all, yet Titch was bombarded, primarily through Loopy Lotto.

Dan nods, pleased and unsurprised. He explains that Titch sounds classically, enticingly, 'sub-prime'.

'Sub-prime is the golden egg,' Dan says. 'If, as a direct marketer, you can identify sub-prime characteristics, you can do very well.'

Dan says the vast majority of all junk mail – be it loans or otherwise – is directed at the sub-prime market: 'The best thing you can tell a client is that you can accurately identify sub-prime individuals. Which is why, when people are asked to fill in lifestyle surveys, they'll often see questions like, "Have you ever experienced difficulty getting credit?" or "Have you ever missed a mortgage payment?" Those are the sorts of triggers that will identify you as potentially sub-prime. It's valuable information.'

It is slightly chilling to realize there are rational, functional people up there employed to spot, nurture and exploit those down here among us who are irrational and can barely cope. If you want to know how stupid you're perceived to be by the people up there, count the unsolicited junk mail you receive. If you get a lot, you're perceived to be alluringly stupid.

A few weeks later I have coffee at Portcullis House with the Labour MP Chris Bryant. He's a member of the Treasury Select Committee, a group of MPs who are trying to investigate the credit-card industry.

'We all know they target the people who are just bumping along,' he says, 'who don't read the small print and don't realize the extortionate interest rates they're paying. We know they use aggressive marketing techniques to persuade those people to take out loans that they often don't understand and simply can't afford.'

'Do any credit-card companies ever admit to this?' I ask.

'Of course not,' says Chris. Then he pauses and says, 'Have you heard of this thing called Mosaic?'

Chris says he doesn't know much about Mosaic, only that it is some computer program. He says he's heard that the credit-card junk-mail departments have grown to rely on Mosaic when determining whom to shower. Apparently, he says, if you type a postcode into Mosaic it'll tell you if the person living at that house wears Burberry, or drinks Coke or white wine, or whatever.

Then Chris moves his chair slightly closer to mine.

'The Tories have Mosaic,' he says. 'They're using it to decide who to target with *their* junk.'

'Are they?' I reply, darkly.

What Chris doesn't tell me – and I only find out later – is that Labour has Mosaic too.

TORIES USE CONSUMER HABITS TO TARGET VOTERS

The contents of voters' shopping baskets are being studied by both main political parties to help them prepare 'bespoke' campaigns in the coming election. The programme was developed in the US where the Republicans' more skilful use of consumer information to target voters is credited with helping George Bush win.

Drinkers of Coors beer, for example, were more likely to vote Republican. Those with a taste for brandy, on the other hand, were found to be Democrats. Labour strategists [admitted] that the party was also using Mosaic.

Independent on Sunday – 6 February 2005

The article goes on to explain how Mosaic is even influencing the Tories' dissemination of their message. For instance, they intend to post their anti-immigration leaflets to households deemed, via Mosaic, to be intolerant of outsiders, but they won't bother sending those leaflets to the more cosmopolitan Tory voters. I wonder: if Chris Bryant was right about Mosaic's influence on the credit-card junk-mailers, what was it about the Richard Cullen's lifestyle that made him seem a suitable target?

I leave a message with the Mosaic people, who turn out to be a company called Experian. Their press officer, Bruno, calls me back. Over the phone he eulogizes Mosaic. He says it is incredibly accurate and used by everyone, more than fifty thousand businesses, including many credit-card companies.

I tell him I still don't quite understand what it does.

'I'll give you a demonstration,' Bruno replies. 'Give me a postcode.'

'Ah,' I say.

I scrabble frantically around my notes until I find Richard Cullen's postcode – the postcode shared by the twenty or so households on the Cullens' street.

'Uh ... BA14 ...' I begin, making it sound like I've just invented a postcode at random.

I hear him type it into his computer.

The Cullens, it turns out, belong to Mosaic's Group B 11: 'Happy Families: Families Making Good'. These are 'older people on middle incomes . . . not high fliers up career ladders of large conglomerates'. Neighbourhoods like this are 'hardly centers of intellectual or aesthetic style'. Happy Families are likely to be interested in adverts for financial products'.

'This is a culture,' concludes Mosaic, 'that is keen to take advantage of easy credit.'

I later discover that a fledgling incarnation of Mosaic called Acorn, which is also used by some credit-card companies, says of Richard Cullen's postcode: 'The interest in current affairs is low. They are educated to a low degree.' (Acorn was invented by the creator of Mosaic – Professor Richard Webber – but it is owned and operated by a company called CACI, and not by Experian.)

Then Bruno types my postcode into Mosaic.

'Wow!' he says. 'You're a Global Connector. Roman Abramovich is a Global Connector too.'

Bruno is clearly impressed.

'We bought before the boom,' I explain, slightly embarrassed.

'Not many *Guardian* journalists are Global Connectors,' says Bruno.

'My street isn't *that* nice,' I say.

'Well, if we've got it wrong you're the exception that proves the rule,' says Bruno a little defensively.

He reads out my profile. Nowhere does it say that we Global Connectors are likely to take advantage of easy credit, nor will we be interested in adverts for financial products.

The reason I don't get nearly as much credit-card junk mail as Richard Cullen did – even Titch doesn't – is that our postcode – N1 – suggests affluence. If I lived in a downmarket postal area, one more befitting Titch's characteristics, he wouldn't have been filtered out by Mosaic. He'd have been deluged.

Bruno invites me to Experian's London offices. I've never heard of them. It turns out that they're not only the power behind Mosaic, they are also Britain's biggest credit-reference agency, with files on forty million people in Britain. Bruno gives me directions. I should walk down Park Lane, he says, turn into Curzon Street, and after a hundred and fifty yards I'll see Leconfield House.

'Apparently it used to be MI5 headquarters,' says Bruno, 'which is very appropriate, I suppose.'

'You've taken over MI5's old building?' I repeat, slightly aghast.

He laughs. 'Yes,' he says.

Leconfield House was indeed MI5 HQ – between 1945 and 1976. And you can tell. It has no street number. Leconfield House is not number anything, Curzon Street. Inside, Experian's offices are all beige and pine, like an airport hotel. Bruno arrives with another man – Professor Richard Webber, 'the father of geodemographics'. This is the man who invented Mosaic and Acorn too.

It isn't my imagination. As we walk to Conference Room A, Professor Webber is looking me up and down, categorizing me on the spot.

'You're wearing training shoes,' he says, slightly baffled, because they don't quite fit with the rest of my clothes.

'I walked here,' I explain. 'I need comfortable shoes for walking.'

'Hm,' says Professor Webber.

Professor Webber's work – profiling and categorizing the lifestyles of the nation – began in the 1970s when he was commissioned by Liverpool City Council to design a computer program that might explain certain nuances of geographical deprivation. Why were some poor areas prone to rioting when others weren't? It turned out that some Liverpool ghettos had preponderances of 'ethnics, drug issues, single parents, low levels of education', whereas others had 'high fertility, high church attendance', and so on. Beefeater Gin was shown to be particularly popular in certain areas.

'Until then,' Professor Webber says, 'nobody knew the connection between neighbourhoods and consumption.'

It wasn't long before the private sector saw the potential.

Ever since, the Professor has been tallying and perfecting, buying up databases from the DVLA, the electoral roll, the British Crime Survey and so on, and augmenting this data with Experian's own lifestyle surveys.

'Which Mosaic category do you fall into?' I ask the Professor.

' "Cultural Leadership",' he says.

'Are you a typical Cultural Leader?' I ask him.

'Yes,' he says.

Cultural Leadership: 'These [highly fastidious] people are assured, secure and very discriminating.

They spend their abundant wealth very carefully. They value the privacy of their homes and home life.'

It doesn't sound like any credit-card companies will be bombarding Professor Webber's home with junk. Mosaic's lifestyle data (Professor Webber writes the text himself) is often really quite impolite. For instance, when people within the category known as 'Welfare Borderlines' purchase cosmetics, they are 'likely to be striking accessories rather than means for displaying natural beauty'. The Professor has, however, been most glowing about his own people, the Cultural Leaders.

I tell Bruno and Professor Webber about Richard Cullen's suicide. I suggest that families like the Cullens are bombarded with junk because the direct-marketing departments of the lenders are guided by Mosaic pointers such as: 'likely to be interested in adverts for financial products . . . keen to take advantage of easy credit' and Acorn pointers like 'educated to a low degree'. In the mathematical world of the credit industry's computer lifestyle calculations it strikes me that a consensus had been formed about the Cullens. The family needed the money but because they owned their own home there was something to seize if needs be. And they weren't smart enough to read the small print and spot the trap they were being beckoned into.

For a moment Bruno seems unsure how to respond to this. My impression is that he doesn't want to downplay Mosaic's significance, but neither does he want to admit that his company's computer program played a role – however peripheral – in a suicide. So he shrugs and says, yes, some credit-card companies use Mosaic, but they use their own files too.

Before I met Professor Webber I fancifully imagined him as a Caractacus Potts, a madcap inventor filled with sorrow at how the private sector had hijacked his brilliant machine. But when I ask him if he's alarmed by any of Mosaic's current uses, he says the opposite is true. He wishes the public sector were efficient enough to use Mosaic more.

'Our country,' he says, 'would be better organized if they did.'

But this is beginning to change, says Bruno. For example, TV Licensing are using Mosaic to choose which areas to target with their vans.

Before I leave, Bruno cranks up his laptop and gives me a slideshow of 'Industrial Grit' type streets – long red-brick terraces, some with boarded-up newsagents. This morning Robert Kilroy-Silk announced his decision to stand for the Veritas Party in the Erewash constituency in Derbyshire in the upcoming general election. Bruno says Kilroy and Erewash are so perfect a match he wouldn't be surprised if Mosaic had been deployed to make the choice.

'Erewash has a remarkable preponderance of Industrial Grit,' explains Professor Webber. 'Home owners, no welfare dependency, no ethnics.'

'They've never been abroad,' adds Bruno. 'Maybe they went to Derby or Nottingham once but they came back in disgust . . .'

(Later, Robert Kilroy-Silk's office tells me that they don't use Mosaic.)

My lasting memory of my afternoon at Experian is Professor Webber and I, a Cultural Leader and a Global Connector, sitting inside these mysterious former MI5 headquarters in the heart of Mayfair, imperiously scrutinizing, via a computer slideshow, the Industrial Grit of Erewash.

As we looked at the slides I asked Professor Webber if he considered himself an academic, but he laughed scornfully and said he was a taxonomist. He said, 'I like putting things into categories. Taxonomy is less authoritarian than academia.'

But Mosaic is packed with the Professor's opinions

and judgements – a subjective mindset that is guiding countless credit-card companies and leading to Happy Families being swamped with offers of easy credit.

Of course Bruno was right that no company will rely solely on Mosaic – but the computer program is surely indicative of the way things are done inside the whirring, mathematical, computer world of credit-card marketing.

'You've probably got enough for a book,' said Bruno as I left that afternoon, which I presume was his way of saying, 'Don't call me again.'

According to the National Consumer Council, one in five people are borrowing money just to pay household bills, and one in four are struggling to meet their repayments. Half a million people in Britain have 'crippling debts on their credit cards'.

Advice services such as Debt Free Direct – who try to help people like Richard Cullen – say they received 275% more calls per day in December 2004 than they did a year earlier. A quarter of those in debt are receiving treatment for stress, depression and anxiety. Britain's bailiffs are enjoying 70% more work than they did two years ago.

Wendy Cullen is annoyed with Debt Free Direct. In the weeks before her husband's suicide, he phoned them countless times for help but, she says, 'They did sod all, excuse my language. They'd phone back and say, "He hasn't sent us the right information." And I'd reply, "I *saw* him send the right information." '

Wendy says that had Debt Free Direct been more helpful her husband would be alive today.

I call Andrew Redmond of Debt Free Direct. He says they're required by law 'to get all this verification. The creditors want proof that the person in question cannot afford to pay more than they say they can afford.'

Andrew says they've been fighting this for years.

'This,' he says, 'is a classic example of a case when a simplification of the process might have averted a tragedy. We had several conversations with Richard Cullen, and we offered the best advice that we could, but it was too little too late.'

Debt Free Direct have transcripts of all the conversations between them and Richard Cullen. In these transcripts – they say – you can read his continual pleas for help. And then you can read the advisors' responses – that they can only help if he can provide this verification, and then that verification, and then the last transcript is the phone call from Christopher Cullen saying that Richard has been found dead.

These days, only 40% of calls made to debt-advice

centres are answered. 60% of the time the centres are so busy the phone just rings and rings.

I phone Barclays to see if someone will talk to me about Richard Cullen.

'I don't think anyone will comment on this at all,' says the first press officer I speak to. 'Someone will get back to you but I really don't think this is something we'll be able to help you with.'

I ask the second press officer if there's anything to be learnt from Richard Cullen's suicide. He says, 'We did lend to Richard Cullen. That was clearly a poor decision. We should have shared data better within the bank. We did get it wrong with Richard Cullen. But we have learnt from this. We are now sharing data better within the bank.'

Is Mosaic used within Barclays as a way to target certain people with junk?

'It is true to say that Mosaic and systems like Mosaic are used by the direct-marketing departments to make our marketing as efficient as possible,' he replies. 'We want to get as few pieces of paper out as possible with the most number of responses. That is the very specific area in which we do use Mosaic – to target people who are likely to respond to direct mail.'

'And Mosaic pointers like "keen to take advantage of easy credit"?' I say.

'Yeah, we would see those as pointers,' he says. 'However, this doesn't mean that the credit-card companies will be willing to lend to that customer. Because we mail to someone in no way suggests that we are willing to lend to that person.'

The third Barclays press officer I speak to says the problem with Richard Cullen was that at the time he didn't *seem* to be in trouble. He was making his repayments. What nobody knew – he says – was he was achieving this by borrowing on other cards.

'Richard Cullen should have asked for help,' he says.

Of course he asked for help, repeatedly, with Debt Free Direct. But they were required by the creditors to make Richard Cullen jump through such complex hoops that they just couldn't help him in time.

I call Wendy Cullen to see if there's any news. She says things are bad. Some credit-card companies have written off the debts, for the sake of good public relations, but others haven't. Morgan Stanley and the RBS, in particular, are being worryingly silent, she says. Wendy's house, and her £500 car, and the caravan, remain at risk.

Just before I phoned, Wendy opened a letter from the credit-card company MBNA. She assumed it was about the debts. Richard had three MBNA cards and sheets of MBNA credit-card cheques, which he used to pay his Goldfish minimum repayments. Wendy knows this because she found the stubs stuffed behind the washing machine a few days ago when it was pulled out for repairs. There they were, in Richard Cullen's neat handwriting: 'G/Fish £172.53.' And so on.

But the letter she received from MBNA today was something different. It read:

> *Dear Mr Cullen*
> *Let's face it most of us encounter financial problems at some stage in our lives. All it takes sometimes is a little bit of bad luck.*

The letter goes on to offer Richard Cullen, who has now been dead for three months, a £15,000 loan. ('10.9% APR variable. Loans are secured on residential property.')

'Just imagine,' the letter concludes, 'this could give you a much needed light at the end of that dark tunnel.'

In 2004, MBNA's profits were one and a half times that of McDonald's.

The Cullens are beginning to piece together the minutiae of the mess Richard got himself into. They've found credit-card statements stuffed in drawers and behind wardrobes all over the house. Wendy says I can come down and look at them.

While I'm sitting there, I hear a key in the front door. It is Christopher.

'Did you hear the radio?' he says. 'Barclays has just announced its highest-ever profits. £4.5 billion. £761 million from Barclaycard.'

Wendy lights another cigarette.

'Did your father have a Barclaycard?' I ask.

'Three,' says Christopher.

'You'd think that would have triggered something off in Barclays' computers,' says Wendy.

'And on top of that,' says Christopher, 'Barclays gave him a £6,000 loan.'

'Oh my God!' says Wendy. 'I didn't know that.'

'Which they upped to £13,000,' says Christopher. 'That's £20,000 in repayments over sixty months. That's just that one loan.'

'How did they let him do that?' says Wendy. 'He

must have been crazy!' She pauses. 'Barclays shouldn't have done that,' she says.

Christopher drives me to his house to look at the statements. There are half a dozen files thick with them. There's a Jiffy bag too, filled with sliced-up credit cards, cut in half when Richard Cullen finally admitted the problem to his wife. MBNA, Goldfish, Tesco, Amex, Frizzell, et cetera, all sliced up.

A typical page of a Richard Cullen credit-card statement reads like this:

Alliance and Leicester
Interest charged: £71.07
Late fee: £25
Overlimit fee: £25

There are thousands and thousands of pounds' worth of these £25s, when you add them up.

Then there are letters too, like this from Barclay-card:

According to our records your Barclaycard
history has been excellent and we have
consequently enrolled you in our Guaranteed

Acceptance Masterloan Programme. This
means we have set aside £7000 for your
immediate access without an application or any
questions whatsoever.

And then, later, another letter from Barclays:

Dear Mr Cullen,
We regret that we have been unable to pay
the following, as there were insufficient funds in
your account:
Payment in favour of Frizzell for £554.09
Payment in favour of Barclaycard for
£339.06
Your account has been debited £30 which is
the fee charged when we are unable to make
payments due to insufficient funds.

This letter did not come from a human being. A
computer, with the printed signature J Smith, churned
it out. There are a number of identical ones – signed
by J Smith – dating back to 2002. How can Barclays
say Richard Cullen didn't seem to be in trouble, when
payments were being declined from one corner of
Barclays to another? At one point, Richard Cullen

went 17p over his Lloyds limit. He was charged £20 for this, and then the interest on that £20.17, and so on.

And then, finally, in the last weeks of his life, scores of letters like this:

Your failure to pay your arrears of £166.04, despite our reminders and offers of assistance, has forced us to withdraw your credit line and take steps to inform the credit reference agency.

The statements tell the story of a man who thought he could beat the credit-card companies at their own game but discovered that he couldn't. He was telling the truth about his absence of secret vices. In the last year of his life almost every payment on every page of every statement was to a different credit-card company. The odd exception was nothing: a £13 subscription to a gardening magazine, and so on.

But he had lied about one thing. Richard Cullen, at the time of his death, didn't owe £30,000. He owed £130,000.

I call Keith Tondeur of Credit Action, which monitors our spiralling debt problem. I tell him what Wendy had said about how hard it used to be for people like them to get loans.

'That's right,' he says. 'Thirty years ago you'd go to your local bank manager. He'd say, "A thousand pounds? You must be joking. I'll give you three hundred." We go into banks looking for the best advice but I know one chief executive who describes his branches as "shops". We treat our bank managers like we treat our doctors. They say, "Ah, you'll need to buy some insurance with that, sir." And we believe them. But in fact we're just being sold things. And this is an industry that's self-regulating. Why is that?'

Later I hear the story of why it takes three days for an electronic transfer to clear. Transfers used to *really* take three days to clear, in the days they were delivered by carrier pigeon, or whatever. But now, in this computer age, they take a nanosecond to clear, but they keep the three-day rule going so they can accrue three days of interest. The banks make tens of millions from these wheezes.

In October 2003 Matthew Barrett, the CEO of Barclays, was called before the Treasury Select Committee. He was asked about the small print. Even though the base interest rate had gone down to 3.5%, buried away in the small print was the revelation that Barclaycard was charging 17.9% interest.

'The small print,' Matthew Barrett admitted to the committee, 'is an eye test for sure.'

Then he added, 'I do not borrow on credit cards. It is too expensive.'

I phone Barclays again and speak with a press officer. I quote him his CEO's statement, that the 'small print is an eye test for sure'. He laughs and says, 'That sounds like Matthew.'

Then he turns serious and says, in terms of the small print, they have made 'huge steps forward in the past twelve to eighteen months. All the credit-card companies have taken out the really important bits from the small print and put them in big letters in the summary box.'

This sounded comforting. Or – at least – it did until the day I attend the International Direct Marketing Fair at Earls Court, West London.

This is the junk-mail industry's annual convention. Here, I discover what looks to me like a small, clever trick regarding a credit-card company and its small print. I discover this trick in the brightly coloured location of the Post-it Note stand.

Even though a sign near the door at Earls Court reads '62% of consumers agree with the statement "I enjoy going through my post" ', the mood here is undeniably panicky. Sue Baker, the PR lady in charge of the event, had told me over the phone, 'People are really worried.' More and more consumers are ticking the no box. They don't want their details passed to third parties.

'The list is severely compromised,' said Sue.

An article in today's *Direct Marketing International* magazine doomily predicts, 'In a couple of years there will be no cold telemarketing industry in Norway. Could this happen here? Well, wake up! It *is* happening.'

6.8 million British people – the article continues – have so far signed up to the telephone preference service, which filters out cold calls.

Everyone is here, from the brokers and profilers, like Mosaic and Baby Marketing, to the myriad businesses that provide the free gifts contained within junk. There's a stand displaying sticks of seaside rock that say 'First Direct – The Time Has Come To Suck It And See'.

The idea is that if someone is sent a sweet, they will be more likely to take out a loan.

*

Like a child I am drawn to the bright colours of the Post-it Note stand, where Post-it Notes of all the colours of the rainbow are displayed within glass cabinets like rare jewels.

'Ever thought about using a Post-it Note on a direct mail piece?' asks their publicity material. 'Studies show that machine-applying a printed Post-it Note can increase your response rate by 18%.'

I ask Peter, who runs the stand, how it works. He shows me a recent piece of junk mail from Capital One. It consists of an offer letter from the credit-card company, outlining all the terms and technicalities, the APRs and the extra charges. Stuck on the front is a bright-yellow Post-it Note, which reads:

This week I will . . .
   Exercise.
   Eat Healthily.
Sort out my finances. Call Capital One on 0800 . . .

'See?' says Peter. 'The letter has all the technical details. You throw the letter away and keep the Post-it Note!'

'Huh,' I say.

So the devil is in the detail, you chuck the devil in the bin and all you're left with is a friendly, brightly coloured Post-it Note with a number to call. It seems that whenever new regulations are forced on the banking industry, someone springs into action and devises a clever new idea that might legally avoid them.

I call Richard Holmes, a spokesperson for Capital One. He says, 'By using a Post-it Note, we are attempting to highlight the key issue for potential customers which is to contact Capital One. This initiative in no way seeks to detract from the importance of the terms and conditions which have to be read and signed by anyone applying for a card.'

An image keeps popping into my head. It's the old days. A customer in need sits down with their manager who says, 'A thousand pounds? You must be crazy! I'll give you three hundred.'

I wonder: is there some economic sage out there who effectively invented the new way – someone who drew up a utopian image where banks would fall over one another to loan money to whoever wanted it?

And so I call Lord Griffiths of Fforestfach. He's the Vice Chairman of Goldman Sachs International, a former director of the Bank of England, and once the head of Margaret Thatcher's Domestic Policy Unit. I'd been told that if anyone could answer that question, he could.

I ask him if this whole mess can be traced back to one man. I expect him to say something like, 'Oh, no, it's far more complicated than that. It is a gradual shift. Nobody is to blame.'

But he doesn't. Instead, he says, 'I hate to say it, but I was one of the people who argued strongly in favour of it.'

'When was this?' I ask.

'December 1970,' he says. 'At that time the banks were a classic cartel, very much a middle-class preserve, and I believed that the democratization of credit had to be a good thing. Everyone in principle should have access to credit.'

So in December 1970, he says, he wrote a paper for the Institute of Economic Affairs advocating a revolution in banking. The report – *Competition in Banking* – concluded: 'The only way in which to make banking a competitive industry is to remove *all* obstacles to potential new entrants into the industry.'

It was, by all accounts, a key factor in the subsequent deregulation of UK banking.

It becomes obvious during my conversation with Lord Griffiths that he's come to believe he's inadvertently unleashed some kind of monster. He says he never could have predicted 'the dynamism' with which the lenders would pursue his ideas.

'The dynamism,' he says. 'The innovation.'

I've never heard these words uttered with such sadness.

'I don't think anyone would have foreseen how innovative and aggressive and competitive the financial services would become in their techniques,' he says. 'The whole lot of them are to blame.' He pauses. 'I'm not advocating a return to the status quo. But the pendulum has swung much too far.'

Now Lord Griffiths has just published a new report – *What Price Credit?* – which has this somewhat apocalyptic conclusion: 'The sheer scale of consumer debt [£1 trillion] has made millions of households extremely vulnerable to shocks to the economy ... such as oil price rises, acts of terrorism and wars ... Debt is a time-bomb for the fifteen million people who struggle with repayments.'

I tell Lord Griffiths about Richard Cullen's suicide and he sighs.

'I had a friend,' he replies. 'A clergyman. I met him for dinner one night. He was suffering from cancer. He broke down over dinner and confessed to me that he had thirty-two credit cards. He said he was using each card to pay off the charges on the others. He told me about the shame he felt. You could just sense the emotional pressure. I'm no doctor . . .'

Lord Griffiths pauses and says, 'He died soon afterwards.'

Then he says that a friend of his recently compared the credit-card industry to slavery – that the lenders are the new slave masters, and the borrowers are the slaves.

I ask Lord Griffiths if he's bombarded with credit-card junk mail and he says, 'Oh yes. I probably get one every fortnight.'

I say that the Cullens were sometimes getting three or four a day.

'Hm,' he says. 'I would call one a fortnight bombardment.'

As I write this, in mid-April 2006, the homeless charity Centrepoint has published a report revealing that almost a quarter of homeless youngsters surveyed have been sent letters from credit-card companies urging them to apply for loans, with interest rates as high as 29%. Somehow, it seems, the list brokers have been able to buy up the names of young people living in hostels and halfway houses.

Since I began writing this article, in January, I have paid Visa about £300 in interest and minimum repayments. I keep thinking I should pay my Visa debts off in full and slice the card up. But I haven't bothered. This is because – like millions of us – I am lazy and stupid. It seems to me that banks like bad customers.

On 26 April, Wendy and two of her children arrive at Salisbury Coroner's Court to hear the verdict. The coroner says the cause of death was carbon-monoxide poisoning: an 85.7% saturation.

'I can tell you, Mrs Cullen, that is very high,' he says. 'That concludes the post-mortem evidence. I am satisfied that his intention was to take his own life. Can I also say, Mrs Cullen . . .'

Wendy is hoping he's about to say something critical of the credit-card companies. But instead he says, 'thank you for coming. By gathering here together we do right by your husband. I formally close the inquest.'

There is one piece of good news. The credit-card companies have all written off the debts now.

'It makes me sad how easy it was for them to write it off,' one of Richard's daughters tells me in the corridor outside.

Epilogue

After spending five months researching Richard Cullen's suicide, I decided to write a book about the credit industry. I had big plans. I'd do to credits what Eric Schlosser did to burgers in *Fast Food Nation*. I'd eviscerate them! I set to work straight away.

I abandoned the idea three months later. The thing is, fast food makes for exhilarating reading. Cows are slaughtered. Migrant workers are horribly injured. Nothing like that happens in the credit-card business. Statisticians sit behind computers. And they're not exciting people. They are – by and large, and no offence to them – boring. I abandoned the idea because I didn't want to write a book about boring people. If you have the ambition to become an evil Bond-style villain and take over the world, the first thing you should do is develop a boring personality. Don't act like Blofeld, monocled up and permanently stroking a fluffy cat. We journalists love writing about eccentrics. We hate writing about boring people. It makes *us* look bad: the duller the interviewee, the duller the prose. I guess that's the problem with solipsistic journalists who care about the quality of their writing.

There was, however, one area of the credit industry

that was fascinating to research: debt collectors. It turned out that societies across the world have developed unique, culture-specific ways to scare the hell out of people who owe money.

In Spain (the only country in Europe where publicly humiliating debtors falls within the law), debt collectors dress in frock coats and top hats and silently follow debtors down the street. They follow them into restaurants and just stand there and point and stare.

In Taiwan, where Aids education is lacking, collection agencies employ people with HIV to follow debtors around and hug them until they agree to pay.

I think the best time and place to be a debtor was in ancient China, where the custom was for the creditor to turn up on the debtor's doorstep and commit suicide so he could pursue him in the afterlife.

That sounds to me like a pretty sweet deal for the debtor.

And, actually, a comparatively good place to be a debtor is here and now, in the Western world. Richard Cullen may have been bombarded by persistent calls from collectors just before Christmas 2004, a month before he committed suicide, but at least the only weapon in their armoury was psychology. At least the days of violence are coming to an end. That's why these are boom times for psychologists employed by collection agencies to teach collectors to be less threatening and more manipulative.

Before I abandoned my credit-card book I signed up for an 'Online Seminar – simultaneously at your PC & telephone line' called 'The Art of Persuasion: Advanced Techniques For Top Debt Collectors'.

It cost me $200, which I paid for with my credit card.

The teacher was a Chicago woman called Debra Ciskey. Across the world collectors (and me) listened to Debra's lecture down our telephone lines whilst interacting with her via a chat box.

'OK,' Debra began. 'What I want you to do is type into the chat box your definition of the word persuasion. Come on. Don't be shy! How do you define persuasion?'

To my surprise, the chat box filled with the sweetest definitions of persuasion I could imagine.

'Persuasion means listening,' typed Denise, a debt collector in Mississippi.

'Providing a win/win situation!' typed Patty, a debt collector in Ohio.

What delightful debt collectors, I thought.

'Those are great answers,' Debra said, before knocking the stuffing out of our humane instincts.

Three hours in, and we were husks of our former selves. We'd been taught to think of debtors' 'sob stories' as 'interference', like the kind of static you get on a bad phone line.

'Debtors don't hear what you're saying because their emotions are getting in the way,' she said, and onto our computer screens came a pictorial representation of debtors' emotions. It was a squiggly line, marked 'Interference'.

'Oh, those sob stories!' Debra laughed. ' "We've got cancer! We can't pay!" They have their *really* sad stories and they *really* want to tell us all about it! Maybe we have to be their audience because nobody has called them for a month! And here we are, trying to get through our Process, and these people are messing up our Process. What can we do about that?'

Actually, Debra seemed very nice. Her laugh after 'Oh, those sob stories!' was not at all heartfelt. It was perfunctory, as if she was reading a script that said in parentheses 'laugh in derisive way'. It felt like we were all slightly reluctant players in this necessary game of dehumanizing ourselves and the debtors.

'So how do we deal with sob stories?' Debra said. 'This is how. Say to them, "It must be rough to be in your situation. I'm here to help you. Help me understand your situation." ' This, Debra explained, is a 'pattern interrupt'. Meaning: sideswipe the debtor by saying something unexpectedly kind. Pretend to care.

'Deep down in our hearts we don't really care what their situation is,' Debra said. 'We haven't got space in our hearts. But we have to make them *think* we care.'

They'll be flabbergasted that a debt collector has shown kindness. Their brain-engines will judder and they'll be left nonplussed. And then, before they have a chance to regain their balance, we zap them with another of our brilliant new secret weapons: 'Future pacing'.

'Future pacing,' Debra explained, is ' "the process of shaping a desired behaviour in a future situation by mentally rehearsing it and pre-negotiating the outcome for an automatic response".' She laughed and said, 'That sounds a little esoteric, right? All it means is use language to get people to think the way you want them to think. Help the consumer visualize himself keeping his promise to pay. Say, "You said the post office is right around the corner from your office, right? It's important that you walk from your office on Friday to the post office and put the cheque in the mail. OK? You'll do that, right?" '

Debra said if we put it that way, they will involuntarily play a movie in their heads. In the movie they'll take that walk from their office to the post office. They'll put the cheque in the mail. And once they've played that movie in their heads we'll 'see the cheques come in a lot quicker, because that's how brains work'.

There was one final exercise. This was the last thing we debt collectors needed to practise, now we had learnt to 'keep emotion out of it' so we didn't 'rise to the bait' of the 'heartbreakers who want to wrap you up in their sad, sad stories'.

'They say they have no money,' said Debra. 'In fact they only *think* they have no money.'

She paused, allowing this riddle to linger.

Then she explained: all we needed to do was remind them that they could easily get hold of the money they owed by taking out a credit-card loan, or a student loan, or a bank loan, or a consolidation loan, or a second mortgage.

So here was a perfect end to our call: 'Well, Chuck, I think we have hit on a solution today. I want to help you get into that fishing tournament. So why don't we get a credit-card loan, and use the money to settle up this bill on your boat. I know you would rather win that tournament in a boat that was completely paid for, so you can have full bragging rights.'

It turned out that every one of Debra's strange,

Jon Ronson

sociopathic-sounding techniques – 'Future pacing',
'Pattern interrupt', that stuff about sob stories being a
squiggly line, all those things designed to make us see
the debtor as some kind of clogged-up, malfunctioning
machine – were the invention of one man.

His name is Richard Bandler.

I decided to track Richard Bandler down.

6. THE SOCIOPATH MIND GURU
AND THE TV HYPNOTIST

It is a Friday in April and you'd think some evangelical faith-healing show was occurring in the big brown conference room of the Ibis Hotel in Earls Court, West London. The music is pumping and the six hundred delegates are ecstatic. And it's true that there are lots of damaged people here who've come to be healed. But this is no faith-healing show. The speakers are atheists. And the audience is full of people from British Airways, Virgin Atlantic, British Gas, BT, BUPA, Dixons, the Department of Work and Pensions, Ladbrokes and Transport for London. These people have come to learn how to be better in the workplace. Now the audience jumps, cheering, to its feet. I look behind me. And I see him passing through the crowd looking like Don Corleone, square-jawed and inscrutable: Richard Bandler.

Of all the gurus who thrived during the Californian New Age gold rush of the 1970s, Bandler nowadays has by far the biggest influence, on millions of people, most of whom know nothing about him or his extra-ordinary past. These days nobody bothers much with naked hot-tub encounter sessions, or primal scream-ing, or whatever. But Bandler's invention – NLP (Neu-rolinguistic Programming) – is everywhere.

The training manual we delegates have been handed describes NLP as 'a methodology based on the presup-position that all behaviour has a structure that can be modelled, learned, taught, and changed.'

The rest of the manual is an even more confusing mix of psychobabble and diagrams marked 'submo-dalities' and 'kinesthetics', et cetera. But from what I can gather, NLP is a way of 're-patterning' the human brain to turn us into super-beings – confident, non-phobic, thin super-beings who can sell coals to New-castle and know what people are thinking just by their eye movements. It is the theory that we are computers and can be reprogrammed as easily as computers can. You were abused as a child? That makes you a badly programmed computer who needs a spot of instant reprogramming. Forget therapy: just turn off the bit of the brain that remembers the abuse. You aren't selling enough houses? NLP can instantly reprogram you to become a great salesperson, or public speaker, or whatever. NLP teaches that – like computers – we are a tapestry of telltale visual and auditory clues to what's going on inside our brains. Our winks, our tics, our seemingly insignificant choice of words – it is all a map of our innermost desires and doubts. It is the secret language of the subconscious. NLP can teach the salesperson how to read that map and act accordingly.

Some people hail the way NLP has seeped into training programmes in businesses across the world. Other people say terrible things about NLP. They say it is a cult invented by a crazy man.

I first heard of Richard Bandler, NLP's inventor (he actually co-invented the technique, with the linguistics professor John Grinder), in 2002 when a former US Special Forces soldier told me he'd watched him, two decades earlier, bring a tiny little girl into Special Forces and reprogram her to be a world-class sniper in seconds. Intrigued, I tried to learn more. This is when I heard about the good times, how Bandler's theories were greeted with high praise in the 1970s and 1980s, how Al Gore and Bill Clinton and practically every Fortune 500 corporate chief declared themselves fans, and then there was the descent into the dark side. Reportedly, during the 1980s, the coked-up Bandler had a habit of telling people he could dial a number and have them killed just like that. Then came the murder trial. In 1988 Bandler was tried and acquitted of murdering a prostitute, Corine Christensen. She'd been found slumped over a dining table, a bullet in her head. Her blood was found sprayed on Bandler's shirt. And then there was the renaissance in the form of Bandler's unexpected partnership with the TV hypnotist Paul McKenna, and the fact that they were going to be teaching a course together this week at the Ibis Hotel.

In the end I will get to meet Richard Bandler and Paul McKenna, and extraordinary things will occur when I do, but the road to those meetings will prove to be a rocky one.

Earlier today I had coffee with Sue Crowley. She's been friendly with Paul McKenna for years, since back in the days when he was touring regional theatres making people believe they were kangaroos. Before that he was a DJ – at Top Shop, then Radio Caroline and finally Capital Radio. Back then the idea that he'd one day hook up with Richard Bandler would have seemed as likely as Doctor Fox becoming business partners with L. Ron Hubbard. But, Sue said, 'Paul was like a dog with a bone when he first learnt of Richard. He studied him at seminars. He modelled Richard like nobody's ever modelled anyone before.'

Modelling is a practice at the heart of NLP. This is how McKenna has described Bandler's invention of modelling: 'If someone's got a skill that you want to master, you "model" that skill so that you can learn to do what they do in a fraction of the time it took them. Say someone's a master salesperson. They'll be doing certain things with their body, and certain things with their language. So you "model" that. Study it, break it down, work out the thinking behind it.'

Sue said Paul McKenna was incredibly nervous about approaching Richard Bandler, before he finally did, in 1994, to suggest they go into business together. Since then, NLP has – thanks to McKenna's skills – become bigger than ever, a vast empire that's making everyone millions.

'Paul is an unexpected protégé of Richard's,' Sue said. 'The squeaky clean DJ and the . . . uh . . .' She paused, not knowing which bits of the Richard Bandler life history to mention, in case I didn't know the full extent of the horror. 'The . . . uh . . . Hell's Angel, up for God knows what, CIA . . . But Richard Bandler is a Leonardo of our times. He is one of our living greats.'

Now, 'Purple Haze' booms through the speakers and Richard Bandler climbs onto the stage. He hushes the crowd. They sit down. I am momentarily lost in my thoughts and I remain standing.

'ARE – YOU – GOING – TO – SIT – DOWN – NOW?' hisses a voice, instantly, in my ear. I jump. It is one of Paul McKenna's assistants. I hurriedly sit down.

'I marched up the Amazon,' Bandler tells the audience. 'I threatened gurus to get them to tell me their secrets. They're pretty cooperative when you hold them over the edge of the cliff.'

There is laughter.

'There was one Indian guru,' Bandler continues, 'I was holding him over the edge of a cliff, I said to him, "My hand is getting tired. You have seven seconds to tell me your secrets." Well, he told me them fast and in perfect English!'

I have to say that had I been tried for murder, I would be less forthcoming with the murder gags. Practically every one of Richard Bandler's jokes are murder-, or at least violent-crime, related. I hope – when I finally get to meet him – to ask him about the murder trial, although I'm nervous at the prospect of this.

Suddenly, we hear a loud noise from somewhere outside.

'A ghost,' Bandler says. 'I do have ghosts that

follow me around. And they're angry ghosts. But I don't care. The truth is, the ghosts are more afraid of me than I am of them.'

He is mesmerizing. Two hours pass in a flash. He talks about childhood trauma. He puts on a whiny voice: ' "When I was five I wanted a pony . . . my parents told me I was ugly . . ." Shut the fuck up!'

He gets the audience to chant it: 'Shut the fuck up! Shut the fuck up! Shut the fuck up!'

If you hear voices in your head, he says, tell the voices to shut the fuck up.

'If you suffered childhood abuse, don't go back and relive it in your mind. Once is enough!'

He says psychotherapy is nonsense and a racket: therapists are rewarded for failure. The longer a problem lasts, the more the therapist is paid. Who cares about the roots of the trauma?

'Don't think about bad things!' Bandler says. 'There's a machine inside your brain that gets rid of shit that doesn't need to be there. Use it! I can give myself amnesia. I can just forget.' He clicks his fingers. 'Just like that.'

This seven-day training course is costing delegates £1,500 each. Which means Paul McKenna's company will rake in almost a million pounds for this one week's work. The tea and biscuits may be free but we have to buy our own lunch. For all the hero-worship of McKenna and Bandler, there's still a lot of grumbling about this, especially because whenever we traipse out into the rain to try and find somewhere to eat in this crappy part of town, we're compelled to traipse past Paul McKenna's immaculate chauffeur-driven silver Bentley, number plate 75PM, parked up in the ugly forecourt, waiting to swish Richard Bandler off somewhere unimaginably fancier.

It is lunchtime now. I walk past the Bentley. A delegate sidles up to me.

'You're a very naughty boy!' she says. 'Richard will be very cross with you!'

'What?' I practically yell.

'You kept writing when Richard was talking even though you *know* you weren't supposed to!' she says. 'And you didn't have a smile on your face. Everyone was laughing, but you were scowling.'

I missed yesterday's session, which is perhaps why everyone is so far ahead of me in the frenzied adoration stakes. In fact, earlier today Richard Bandler said he had no unhappy clients. His exact words were, 'The reason why all my clients are a success is that I killed all the ones who weren't.'

Lots of delegates have told me they signed up because of the TV star Paul McKenna but the great revelation has been the man they hadn't heard of: Richard Bandler.

Three of Paul McKenna's NLP-inspired self-help books (*Change Your Life In Seven Days*, *Instant Confidence* – which is dedicated to Bandler – and *I Can Make You Thin*) are currently in the WH Smith Top 10. So that's the therapy side. The NLP Can Do Wonders For Your Business side is thriving too. In fact when I meet Iain Aitken, the managing director of McKenna's company, he says the phobic delegates are becoming the minority now NLP has become so widespread in the business world. I ask Iain what is it about NLP that attracts the salespeople. Bandler, he replies, teaches that everyone has a dominant way of perceiving the world, through seeing, hearing or feeling. If a customer says, 'I see what you mean,' that makes them a visual person. The NLP-trained salesperson will spot the clue and establish rapport by mirroring the language.

'I get the picture,' the NLP-trained salesperson can reply, rather than 'That rings a bell,' or 'That feels good to me.'

*

After lunch, we split into small groups to practise NLP techniques on one another. I pair up with Vish, who runs a property company in the Midlands.

'What did I miss yesterday?' I ask him.

'It was great,' he says. 'We did anchoring. Let me show you how it works.'

Vish moves his chair closer to mine.

'How are you enjoying your time here?' he asks me.

'OK,' I say.

Vish pokes my elbow.

'Brilliant!' he says. 'Did you have a good lunch?'

'It was all right,' I say.

Vish prods my elbow again.

'Fantastic!' he says. 'Have you got kids?'

'A son,' I say.

'Did you have fun with him last weekend?' he asks.

'Yes, I did,' I say.

Vish pokes my elbow.

'Brilliant!' he says. 'Now. Did you notice what I was doing?'

'You were poking my elbow every time I expressed positive feeling,' I say.

'Exactly!' says Vish, although he looks peeved that I spotted the poking, which is supposed to be so subtle as to exist only on the unconscious level.

'Now,' says Vish. 'When I want to sell you something I'll touch your elbow and you'll associate that touch with good feeling, and you'll want to buy. That's deep psychology.' Vish pauses. 'What I really like about NLP is how it can hypnotize and manipulate people. But in a good way.'

I stand up to stretch my legs and I spot Paul McKenna at the front near the stage. Even though I'm still supposed to be doing the small group workshop, I decide to introduce myself. I take a few steps towards McKenna. Instantly, one of his assistants swoops down on me. There are about forty assistants in all, scattered around the room.

'Do you need help?' she asks me.

'No,' I say.

'Have you *finished* the workshop already?' she asks, sarcastically.

'Yes,' I say.

'Well, you must have finished quicker than everyone else because everyone else is still doing it,' she says.

'I'm a journalist and I'm going to talk to Paul McKenna,' I say.

I walk on. Ten steps later, two more assistants appear from nowhere.

'Aren't you joining in?' asks one.

'You're going to miss *all* the benefits,' says the other.

'I'm OK, honestly,' I say.

Another assistant appears.

'Didn't you understand your instruction?' he says. 'Paul explained *three times* that you're supposed to do the workshop for fifteen minutes.'

Finally, exhausted, I reach Paul McKenna. I introduce myself.

'How did you end up in business with Richard Bandler?' I ask him.

'I know!' he says. 'It seems incredible from the outside. But he's one of my best friends . . .' Then he excuses himself to do a spot of speed-healing on an overeater.

An hour later Paul McKenna's PR, Jaime, tells me in the corridor quite sternly that I am not to hang out with Paul or Richard before, between or after sessions because they're far too busy and tired. I can meet them next Wednesday, she says, when the course is over. I go home. I don't think I have ever, in all my life, had so many people try to control me in one single day. Advocates and critics alike say attaining a mastery of NLP can be an excellent way of controlling people, so

I suppose the training courses attract that sort of person. Ross Jeffries, author of *How To Get The Women You Desire Into Bed*, is a great NLP fan, as is Duane Lakin, author of *The Unfair Advantage In Sales*. (Both books advocate the 'that *feels* good to me' style of mirroring/rapport-building invented by Bandler.)

But still, the controlling didn't work on me. Nobody successfully got inside my head and changed – for their benefit – the way I saw NLP. In fact quite the opposite happened. This makes me wonder if NLP even works.

Emails and telephone calls fly back and forth. I tell Jaime the PR that I don't want to be kept away from Richard Bandler during the sessions. Finally it is agreed I can meet him before he goes on stage on Monday.

Things improve. There's a nice, normal delegate here called Nick who teaches executives how to be good public speakers.

'These group things are always a bit creepy,' he says, 'but that isn't the point. The point is that NLP isn't bogus.'

I tell Nick about Vish noticeably prodding me in the elbow.

'Well, he was just doing it badly,' says Nick. 'Honestly. NLP is the most sensible thing out there.'

I corner Paul McKenna and tell him his assistants are driving me crazy.

'You *have* to make them leave me alone,' I say.

He looks mortified, and says they're just overexcited and trying too hard. But, he adds, the course would be a lot worse without them energizing the stragglers into practising NLP techniques on one another.

On stage, Bandler and McKenna cure a stream of delegates of their phobias and compulsions. There's a woman who's barely left her home for years, convinced the heater will turn itself on when she's out and burn the house down.

'Do they pay you to think like this?' asks Bandler. 'It seems like an awful lot of work. Aren't you fucking sick of it?'

The woman says a bossy voice in her head tells her the heater will do this.

Bandler gets her to turn down the knob in her brain that controls the volume of the bossy voice.

Then he gets the bossy voice to tell her, 'If you keep worrying about this heater you're going to miss out everything good in your life.'

This, Bandler explains, is an invention of his called the Swish technique: you take a bad thought, turn it into a radio or TV image and then swish it away, replacing it with a good thought.

'I don't care about you any more, heater, because I want to get my life back,' the woman says, and the audience cheer.

I still don't quite understand the Swish technique, and so I make a mental note to get Paul McKenna to do it on me when I meet him at his house on Wednesday. I have a whole potpourri of bad thoughts I wouldn't mind swishing away.

Yesterday Richard Bandler cured someone who had a fear of doctors. Now he gets him to stand up.

'Are you scared of going to the doctor?' he asks.

'I . . . uh . . . hope not,' the man quietly replies.

'BOO!' shout the audience, only half-good-naturedly.

Suddenly, I feel a poke in my elbow. I spin around. It is Vish. I catch him in the act of giving my elbow a second poke.

'Did that make you feel good?' he asks me.

'It made me feel confused,' I say.

When someone appears cured, Bandler and McKenna seem quietly, sincerely thrilled. I'm sure they derive real pleasure from helping damaged people improve their lives. And the room truly is scattered with NLP success stories. There are the shy salespeople who aren't shy any more, the arachnophobes who swish away their spider phobias and stroke the tarantulas Paul McKenna provides one afternoon.

On stage each day, McKenna is a mix of entertainer and college lecturer. He tells a joke and then he says, 'What was I just doing?'

'REFRAMING!' the audience yell as one. (Reframing is NLP's way of putting a miserable person in a good mood. If someone says, 'My wife's always nagging me,' the NLP-trained therapist will 'reframe' by replying, 'She must really care about you to tell you what she thinks.') It's obvious that making people think they were kangaroos was never going to be enough for McKenna. This is what he loves: being a boffin. A multimillionaire boffin.

I sit in the audience and watch all this, and back at home in the evenings I talk to friends who, it transpires, secretly listen to Paul McKenna's CDs and get cured. I still don't know how it works. Maybe it'll become clear when I ask him to cure me on Wednesday.

There's another speaker here: the life coach Michael Neill, author of *You Can Have What You Want*. One day Michael asks me if I can spot the covert intelligence officers in the audience.

'I'm not joking,' he says. 'There's always one or two.'

'Why?' I ask.

'Most people who want to get inside your brain,' says Michael, moving closer to me, 'have negative reasons.'

Michael tells me about an oil-executive friend who only ever uses NLP for bad, to 'mess people up'. In busy bars his friend frantically 'mismatches'. He sits at a crowded table, uses NLP to establish rapport with strangers and then behaves in the exact opposite way to what he knows would make them feel comfortable. Before long he has the table to himself. Then Michael adds, 'Anyone who knows NLP will have an advantage over anyone who doesn't. My dream is for everyone in the world to know NLP. Then there'd be an even playing field.'

Paul McKenna, standing nearby, comes over. He scans the room. When the six hundred delegates graduate in a few days, they'll be given Licensed NLP Practitioner certificates. Some will set up their own NLP training schools. He says he cannot guard against what happens next.

'Some people teach NLP in a way that makes it sound highly manipulative and coercive,' McKenna says. 'You know, "I will give you power over others." And the people who end up going to those are people with very small penises, frankly. People who think, "Oh my God! I'm not enough! I'm so out of control! Maybe if I learnt how to have power over others I'd be a better person!" So you see that criticizing NLP is like criticizing a hammer.'

I tell him I've read terrible things about NLP on the Internet – how some scientists call it nonsense – and he says, 'I *know* it's not scientific. Some of the techniques will not always work in the same way in a laboratory every time!' He laughs. 'But Louis Pasteur was accused of being in league with the Devil. The Wright brothers were called fraudsters . . .'

Monday. I spot Richard Bandler by the stage, surrounded by fans.

'Wow,' he says, as a woman hands him a rare copy of his book *Trance-formations*. 'That goes for, like, six hundred dollars on eBay.'

'That's where I got it,' the woman replies. He autographs it.

Everything is going fine until someone hands Bandler a blank piece of paper to sign.

'What's this?' he says. 'I just don't sign blank paper.' He pauses. 'I have a thing about it.'

Misunderstanding, the woman hands him different blank paper.

'No, no,' he says. 'I just can't sign blank paper.'

Some of the fans laugh to say, 'How can you hand him blank paper after he's just *told* you he doesn't sign blank paper? Are you *nuts* to expect him to sign blank paper?'

But really it is a strange moment: Richard Bandler has just spent the last few days effortlessly convincing us that phobias are nonsense, and here he is, phobic about signing blank paper.

The moment passes. A woman kisses him and says, 'From one child of the sixties to another.' Bandler laughs and replies, 'They called us the fringe. We're fucking *mainstream* now!' Then I introduce myself, and we go upstairs.

Richard Bandler was born in 1950. He grew up in a rough part of New Jersey. I don't expect him to talk much about his childhood because several profiles say he never does. The one thing known for sure is that he had language problems, and he barely spoke until he was a teenager. So I'm surprised when he says, 'I was a compulsive kid.'

I'm sitting down on a low sofa. He's standing above me.

'When I was a kid I took up archery,' he says. 'I can remember sitting out by the side of the house, until 3 a.m., with just a little light bulb, shooting at a fucking target, over and over until I got it exactly the way it was supposed to be.'

'Where did your compulsiveness come from?' I ask him.

'From being alone most of the time,' he says. 'I had to be self-motivated. My mother was always out working, and my father was violent and dangerous.' He pauses. 'Well, my first father was gone by the time I was five, and he was very violent. My mother later married a guy who was a drunk and a prizefighter in the navy. He was very violent. Broke a lot of my bones. But in the end I won.'

'How?' I ask, expecting him to say something like, 'Look at me now. I'm getting driven around in Paul McKenna's Bentley.'

But instead he says, 'I electrocuted him.'

'Really?' I say.

'I didn't kill him,' he says, 'but I could have.'

'How did you electrocute him?' I ask.

'I waited until it was raining,' he says. 'I got a wire-mesh doormat. I stripped a lamp cord, put it underneath the doormat, put the other end in the keyhole, and put my hand on the switch. When the key went in, I clicked the switch. There was a loud scream. He went over the railing. Six months in the hospital.'

'How old were you?' I ask.

'Ten,' he says.

I remember his advice for people who suffered childhood abuse: 'Just forget about it.' Tell the voices to 'shut the fuck up'. Is NLP Bandler's way of avoiding confronting the demons of his past? Or perhaps it's the opposite. Why else would he spend his life mapping the crazy ways people behave, if not to try to understand the senselessness of his own childhood? I ask him this, and he shrugs and replies, 'I don't think too much about my childhood. I just left it behind me. I moved on.'

The family moved to California, where Bandler became 'a juvenile delinquent. Then I discovered it wasn't the Harley that was scaring people. It was the look in the eye.'

He was diagnosed as a sociopath. 'And, yeah, I am a little sociopathic. But it turns out I *am* right. And my illusions were so powerful they became real, and not just to me.'

He says NLP came to him in a series of hallucinations while he was 'sitting in a little cabin, with raindrops coming through the roof, typing on my manual typewriter.'

This was 1975. By then he was a computer pro-grammer, a twenty-five-year-old graduate of the University of Santa Cruz.

It's surprising to me that Bandler would cheerfully refer to NLP as a sociopathic hallucination that struck a chord with the business world. I'm not sure he's ever been that blunt about it before. But I suppose, when you think about it, there *is* something sociopathic about seeing people as computers that store desires in one part of the brain and doubts in another.

'See, it's funny,' he says. 'When you get people to think about their doubts, notice where their eyes move. They look down! So when sales people slide that contract in, suddenly people feel doubt, because that's where all the doubt stuff is.'

'So where should a salesperson put the contract?' I ask.

'They've got to buy themselves a clipboard!' he says. 'When you ask people to think about things that are absolutely right for them, they look up! So you put the contract on a clipboard and present it to them up here!'

These were the kinds of ideas Bandler was typing in Santa Cruz at the age of twenty-five. The book would eventually be co-written with linguistics professor John Grindler and published under the title *The Structure of Magic*.

Throughout the interview, I'm sitting on a low, dark red leather sofa with Bandler standing above me. Something suddenly dawns on me.

'If I was standing and you were sitting,' I ask, 'would I be forming different opinions of you?'

'Yeah,' he says. 'Of course.'

'So are you deliberately positioning yourself in my hopes and desires eye-line?' I ask.

There's a silence. Bandler smiles to himself.

'No,' he says. 'My leg hurts. That's why I'm standing up.'

The Structure of Magic was a huge hit. '*Time* magazine, *Psychology Today*, all of these people started seeking me out in Santa Cruz,' he says. 'And I started getting interest from places I really didn't expect, like IBM.'

He designed sales-training programmes for businesses across America. They made him rich. He bought a home in Hawaii and a mansion in Santa Cruz. He was hailed as a genius. The CIA and military intelligence squirrelled him in, which is how I first heard of him. Had he really smuggled a tiny girl into Special Forces and got her to 'model' a world-class sniper?

'It wasn't a little girl,' he says. 'It was a ten-year-old boy. And that's not as great as it sounds. You can teach a ten-year-old boy to pretty much do anything.'

But by the early 1980s, things were spiralling downwards for him. His first wife filed for divorce, claiming he choked her. According to a 1989 *Mother Jones* profile, he began to warn associates, 'All I need to do is dial seven digits and with my connections with the Mafia I could have you all wiped out without even batting an eye.'

He became a prodigious cocaine user and he struck up a friendship with a fifty-four-year-old cocaine dealer, James Marino. By 1986 he was living in a house built by Marino. A few doors away lived Marino's girlfriend, Corine Christensen.

In early November 1986, James Marino was beaten up, and he got it into his head that Corine had organized the beating so she could take over his cocaine business. Marino was paranoid, and he infected his friend with the paranoia. Bandler phoned Corine up, recording the conversation: 'Why is my friend hurt? I'll give you two more questions, and then I'll blow your brains out . . .'

Eight hours later, Corine Christensen was shot in

the head at her home, and twelve hours after that Bandler was arrested for the murder.

I've been worried about bringing this up with him. Bandler may be quite brilliant and charismatic but he also seems overbearing and frightening. And although Paul McKenna himself strikes me as likeable, his team of overzealous (literally overzealous) assistants scattered around the hotel are forever eyeing me with suspicion if I appear anything less than completely thrilled. Plus, earlier Jaime the PR cornered me in the corridor and said, 'A few people have reported to me that you've been asking about banking and finance. You aren't going to be writing about how NLP can be misused, are you?'

Then she looked me in the eye and added, 'Some people are concerned.'

And that's just because I was asking about banking! What'll happen if I ask about murder – not the pretend murders Bandler jokes about on stage, but a real one? Still, they aren't in the room now.

'Tell me about the murder trial,' I say.

He doesn't pause at all. He tells me what he told the jury – that James Marino did it. There were two men in the house when Corine was murdered – the famous Richard Bandler and the lowlife James

Marino. Yes, he was there. He lifted her head, which is how her blood ended up on his shirt. Why do I think the police went after him?

'With me, the DA gets to make a big reputation,' he says. 'But if it's some thug drug-dealer you're not going to make any mileage.'

The trial lasted three months. The jury acquitted Bandler after five hours of deliberation. On the stand, Bandler blamed Marino and Marino blamed Bandler. There was no way for the jury to know which of the two was telling the truth. Plus, James Marino was at times an unbelievable witness, frequently changing his story. Sometimes he was upstairs when Bandler shot her, sometimes he was downstairs. Plus, as the *Mother Jones* profile pointed out, who had the greater motive: the man who had been beaten up, or the man who was righteously indignant on behalf of a friend who had been beaten up?

'It took the jury longer to pick a foreman than to decide if I was guilty or innocent,' Bandler says. 'The guy was a convicted felon! We caught him lying, falsifying evidence . . .'

It is at this exact moment that Paul McKenna and the entire upper echelons of his company troop cheerfully into the room.

'The other guy was their stool-pigeon they used to

bust dope dealers!' Bandler is now hollering at me. 'I mean *excuse me*! A lot of very dirty things went on through that trial.'

Earlier today Paul McKenna got a compulsive blusher on stage and cured her of her blush. I am like the blush lady now, sitting on the Chesterfield sofa, Bandler towering over me, yelling about the murder rap, while Paul McKenna and his MD look anxiously on.

I change the subject. I say, half-joking, that being an NLP genius must be awful: 'To know in an instant what everyone's thinking by their winks and tics and barely perceptible sideways glances and eye movements,' I say. 'You must sometimes feel like one of those superheroes, ground down by their own superpowers.'

'Yeah,' Bandler replies, suddenly looking really quite upset. 'It's called the supermarket.'

He pauses.

'You walk into a supermarket and you hear someone say to their kid, "You're never going to be as smart as other kids." And I see the kid's eyes, pupils dilating, and I see the trance going on in that moment . . . It became a burden to know as much as I did. I went through a lot of things to distract myself. I used to just sit and draw all the time. Just draw. Focus on drawing to keep my mind from thinking about this kind of stuff.' And then he goes quiet, as if he is falling into himself.

I suppose people shouldn't judge gurus until they need one. Luckily, I do a bit. And so on Wednesday I use my ninety minutes with Paul McKenna to get him to cure me of my somewhat obsessive, debilitating conviction that something bad has happened to my wife and son when I can't get hold of them on the phone. I've always suffered from this. If I am in America, and I can't reach them on the phone, I become convinced that Elaine has fallen down the stairs, and is lying at the bottom with a broken neck, and Joel is reaching up to grab the flex of a newly boiled kettle. I have panicked unnecessarily about this, over the years, all over the world.

Paul McKenna does Richard Bandler's Swish technique on me. He gets me to picture one of my horrific imaginary scenes. I choose my son stepping out in front of a car.

He spots, from my eye and hand movements, that the mental image is situated in the top right hand of my vision, big, close to my eyes.

'Part of the neural coding where we get our feelings

from, and ultimately our behaviour, comes from the position of these pictures,' he explains. 'Pictures that are close and big and bright and bold have a greater emotional intensity than those that are dull and dim and further away.'

'And Richard Bandler was the first person to identify this?' I ask.

'Yes,' he says.

He chats away to me, in his hypnotic baritone voice, about this and that: his own worries in life, et cetera. Suddenly, when I'm not expecting it, he grabs the space in the air where my vision was, and mimes chucking it away.

'Let's shoot it off into the distance,' he says. 'Shrink the picture down, drain the colour out of it, make it black and white. Make it transparent . . .'

And, sure enough, as the image shoots away, far into the distance, the neurotic feelings associated with it fade too. This is Paul McKenna 're-patterning' my brain. He says this isn't self-help. I don't have to do anything. This is reprogramming, he says, and I am fixed.

'Oh yeah,' he says. 'You don't have to do anything now. It's worked.'

A year passes. I don't have a single paranoid

fantasy about something bad happening to my wife and son. I really am cured.

And so I have to say, for all the weirdness, I become very grateful that Richard Bandler invented NLP and taught it to Paul McKenna.

Visit **www.picador.com** to read more about all our books and to buy them. You will also find features, author interviews and news of any author events, and you can sign up for e-newsletters so that you're always first to hear about our new releases.